ERROR-FREE SOFTWARE

KNOW-HOW AND KNOW-WHY OF PROGRAM CORRECTNESS

Robert Laurence Baber

Translated from the German original by the author

JOHN WILEY & SONS
Chichester · New York · Brisbane · Toronto · Singapore

Error-free Software: Know-how and Know-why of Program Correctness by Robert Baber is a translation from the German book *Fehlerfreie Programmierung für den Software-Zauberlehrling*, published in 1990 by R. Oldenbourg Verlag, Munchen.

Copyright © 1991 by John Wiley & Sons Ltd.
                       Baffins Lane, Chichester
                       West Sussex PO19 1UD, England

Other Wiley Editorial Offices

John Wiley & Sons, Inc., 605 Third Avenue, New York, NY 10158-0012, USA

Jacaranda Wiley Ltd, G.P.O. Box 859, Brisbane, Queensland 4001, Australia

John Wiley & Sons (Canada) Ltd, 22 Worcester Road, Rexdale, Ontario M9W 1L1, Canada

John Wiley & Sons (SEA) Pte Ltd, 37 Jalan Pemimpin 05-04, Block B, Union Industrial Building, Singapore 2057

Library of Congress Cataloging-in-Publication Data:
Baber, Robert Laurence.
    [Fehlerfreie Programmierung für den Software-Zauberlehrling. English]
    Error-free software : know-how and know-why of program correctness / by Robert Laurence Baber ; translated from the German original by the author.
       p. cm. — (Wiley series in software engineering practice)
    Translation of: Fehlerfreie Programmierung für den Software - Zauberlehrling.
    Includes bibliographical references and index.
    ISBN 0 471 93016 4
    1. Computer software—Reliability. 2. Computer software— —Development. I. Title. II. Series.
QA76.76.R44B33 1991
005—dc20   91-12380
                                          CIP

A catalogue record for this book is available from the British Library

Printed in Great Britain by Biddles Ltd, Guildford

CONTENTS

The most important proof rules:

PREFACE

This book is the result of an evolutionary process which took place over a number of years. The contents of this book are based on my seminar for experienced software developers, which I instruct internationally, and on courses which I have taught as an external lecturer in the Informatics Department of the Johann Wolfgang Goethe University in Frankfurt/Main, Germany. These are based, in turn, on my own experience applying this material in commercial software development practice.

The questions posed by participants at my seminar and students have influenced the organization and structure of this book significantly. Also the skepticism about the practical applicability of this material sometimes expressed by experienced software developers and their managers has affected my choices of the content of this work and its presentation.

Most important, however, were the very positive reactions of my students and seminar participants. They motivated me to try to make this subject more understandable and accessible to the software development practitioner. The enthusiasm about this material and the possibilities arising from its consequent practical application expressed at my seminars, lectures, etc. is, in my opinion, a clear indication that this approach to reliable software is both practically feasible and sorely needed. A significant fraction of our software developers – especially the younger ones – is already convinced of the potential of this subfield of software development. Their growing numbers will lead to a rather fundamental change in software development practice in the not too distant future.

I would like to take this opportunity to thank all who have contributed – directly or indirectly, consciously or unknowingly – to this book. Among them are my seminar participants, students, consulting clients and professional colleagues. For the drawing of the software sorcerer appearing in several places in this book I am very grateful to Mrs. José Zwakman. Above all I am much indebted to Drs. Willem Dijkhuis for his valuable advice on all of my major writing efforts. His suggestions led to the title of the original German edition of this book and to the subtitle of the English translation now in your hands.

ROBERT LAURENCE BABER
Landgraf Gustav Ring 5
6380 Bad Homburg v.d.H.
Germany
1990 December

MATHEMATICAL NOTATION

not	Logical (Boolean) function. See Appendix A, section A.1.
or	Logical (Boolean) function. See Appendix A, section A.1.
and	Logical (Boolean) function. See Appendix A, section A.1.
$\Longrightarrow$	Logical (Boolean) function. See Appendix A, section A.1.
$\mathbf{or}_{i=1}^{n}$	The **or** series. See Appendix A, section A.5.
$\mathbf{and}_{i=1}^{n}$	The **and** series. See Appendix A, section A.5.
∎	Marks the end of an example, a definition of a proof rule, etc.
'	Indicates the value of a variable or an expression *before* the execution of a statement. See e.g. sections 2.2 and 2.3.

"   Indicates the value of a variable or an expression *after* the execution of a statement. See e.g. sections 2.2 and 2.3.

{V} S {P}   Means "V is a precondition of the postcondition P with respect to the statement S". See section 3.1.

P^x_E The expression obtained by replacing the variable x in the expression P by the expression (E). See section 3.3.2.

Z   The set of all integers (0, 1, -1, 2, -2, ...). See section 4.4.1.

ε Means "is an element of the set". The expression "nεZ" means, for example, "(the value of) n is an element of the set of all integers" or, more briefly, "the value of n is an integer". See section 4.4.1.

$|x|$ The absolute value of x. If x is negative, then $|x|$ is equal to -x. If x is zero or positive, then $|x|$ is equal to x.

0

THE SORCERER'S APPRENTICES IN THE LAND OF THE RET UP MOC

In 2500 B.C. the Land of the Ret Up Moc was an advanced society in the cradle of civilization. A number of important cities had been founded and active trade, both domestic and foreign, flourished. A construction industry existed in which professionally trained architects and civil engineers played an important role.

Between 2500 and 2400 B.C., a major innovative technical advance was achieved. Suddenly and unexpectedly, a group of civil engineering teachers headed by Akado, a famous and leading architect, developed a new technique for designing the load carrying structures of buildings. By using the new method, much larger buildings could be designed and constructed than had been previously possible. Perhaps even more importantly, considerably less material was required to construct buildings designed in the new way. This resulted in much lower construction costs. Consequently, the demand for new buildings of all types increased very rapidly.

The demand for new building designs increased so much that the already qualified architects who had taken the time to learn the new method could not satisfy their potential customers' requirements. The number of newly trained journeymen and masters who could act as architects' assistants was also insufficient to alleviate the problem. The building materials trade – unwilling to pass up such an interesting opportunity to increase sales – found a "solution": short courses and seminars were developed to train foremen and even construction workers, etc. to draft plans for new buildings. They did not really understand the new scientific basis for their work, of course, but as long as they did not deviate from the detailed rules which they memorized in the courses, the results were more or less acceptable. Approximately a third of the new buildings collapsed during or immediately after construction. The resulting losses were, however, still significantly less than the savings derived from employing the new method. So on balance, this new approach to designing buildings was clearly better than the old way. [Baber, 1982, 1986, 1987, Chapter 0]

After one to two decades the following equilibrium had become established in the construction industry. Most building designers were trained in the short courses outlined above and were correspondingly underqualified for their work. They were quite satisfied with this state of affairs, for it permitted them to start early earning a high income. The royal leadership of Moc was content with this situation, for it minimized the expense of training the building designers. Furthermore, those costs were borne primarily by the building industry, not the government. The building industry's customers were also basically happy, because they could have larger and cheaper buildings than before. Only Akado and his professional colleagues were dissatisfied with the new situation in the building industry. They knew that every collapse was avoidable and that the necessary investment in the proper professional education of building designers would, overall, be less expensive in the long term than the losses caused by the many collapses. In short, in Akado's view, the current approach was better than the previous situation, but truly professional practice – based on a correspondingly challenging and intensive education of the building designers – would be even better.

Akado and his colleagues not only taught civil engineering but also designed new buildings themselves. In sharp contrast to the general Mocsian construction experience, the buildings they designed never collapsed. Sometimes they were asked why not. They described the basis of their calculational method, but the other building designers could not or would not understand their explanations. Almost all customers believed that Akado's success was due solely to chance and luck and, therefore, was not rationally explainable. Because he charged slightly higher fees than the less qualified designers, his better services were not in great demand.

Disappointed about this state of affairs, Akado discussed it occasionally with his best friend, Naram, a famous actor and amateur psychologist. Naram understood completely the attitude of the customers, even though it was clearly irrational, and tried to explain it to Akado. The customers were just ordinary people, not intellectuals, and like almost everyone in the Land of the Ret Up Moc, very religious, even superstitious. They could not understand rational scientific explanations and were suspicious of anyone resorting to them. Consequently, they considered such an approach to planning buildings to be impractical. In Naram's opinion, Akado's approach obviously lacked sorcery and superstition, which were so important in Moc. Naram conceived a magic show for Akado which included all sorts of superstitious incantations, magical formulae, mysterious songs, spells and charms, witch dances, etc. Naram directed rehearsals with Akado and shared several actors' secrets with him. When Naram was satisfied with Akado's theatrical performance, he turned him loose on the customers.

The premiere of Akado's magic show comprised the major part of the dedication ceremony for his next building, a particularly large office complex for the royal government. Akado's performance was a smashing success and potential customers were so impressed that Akado was overwhelmed with new architectural assignments. Several leading priests even became mildly jealous over Akado's partial invasion of their domain. Akado repeated this performance at the appropriate stage of construction of every building which he subsequently designed. With Naram's assistance Akado continually developed his magic show to an ever more dramatic and impressive happening.

No one in Moc really understood sorcery, of course, but everyone believed in it, because it was a fundamental component of the primitive Mocsian religion, culture and mentality. Akado always recited the magic words very impressively and always – without exception – the new building remained standing. The magic worked; so simple was the explanation for the success of the construction project.

At first Akado's conscience bothered him, for he knew that sorcery had nothing to do with the fact that his buildings never collapsed. The magic shows only took time and increased his costs, although only marginally. But he recognized that his friend Naram was right. The customers did not want professional architecture, they wanted building magic. They wanted to believe in it. They wanted reasonable plans for their new buildings, too, of course. Akado gave them both at the same time: building magic and building plans of high quality. He was not acting fraudulently, he was merely "selling" precisely the combination of services which his customers wanted to "buy". Mocsian society needed professional civil engineering and wanted building magic. Akado provided both.

Akado became very famous as a master of building sorcery. As is always the case with a master sorcerer, candidate sorcerer's apprentices soon found their way to him. He took on the best of them and founded the School of Building Sorcery. Naturally he disclosed the true secret of building "magic" to them, because otherwise they would not, after completing their training, be successful and the whole deception would be exposed. Such a misfortune would be detrimental to all concerned: Akado, his building sorcerer's apprentices and, last but not least, the customers, who derived considerable benefit from Akado's method.

The number of apprentices attending the School of Building Sorcery grew rapidly. In order to organize instruction more efficiently, Akado wrote a textbook. His book, *Collapse Free Building Designs – Know-How and Know-Why of Static Soundness*, recorded both the scientific and the magic-theatrical foundations of building sorcery and transmitted them to his pupils. Many later generations of building sorcerers also learned the fundamental principles of their profession from this book.

2400 B. C.

↓

1990 A. D.

In terms of content and organization, the book you are now reading corresponds to the old textbook written by Akado for his apprentices of building sorcery – except for his chapters on magic spells and sayings and performing magic shows. In our modern times these aspects of truly professional software development practice should be superfluous, even though the resulting freedom from errors appears to many to be incredibly magical.

1

INTRODUCTION

1.1 THE PROBLEM: ERRORS IN SOFTWARE

Computer software is still characterized by an unsatisfactorily high error rate. Even though most of the mistakes originally present in newly written software are found and corrected before it is released to the user, the remaining errors still cause unnecessary cost, lost time and effort, inconvenience and annoyance during and long after the implementation of a system. Reports of considerable losses resulting from errors in software continually appear in the press. Even human deaths have been attributed to software errors: Computer controlled systems for medical therapy have administered lethal doses of radiation [Joyce, 1987], [*IEEE Spectrum*, 1987] and of an injection [Thomas, 1988, p. 9].

Computer systems are already so widespread that our society has become completely dependent upon them. Without such data processing systems we would simply be unable to process the majority of today's business transactions. Even in safety critical areas computer systems provide important support (e.g. air traffic control). The growth of such applications in the future will lead to greater demands being placed on the reliability of such systems and of the software and hardware comprising them. The consequences of errors in software will become ever more serious and expensive. If we software developers do not succeed in decreasing *very* substantially and fundamentally the frequency of design errors ("bugs" in our software), the risks associated with computer systems will seriously limit their utilization – and even preclude some otherwise economically justified applications.

We must openly admit – especially to ourselves – that errors in software are avoidable design errors – human errors on the part of the software developer. They are not inherent in the nature of software.

1.2 THE SOLUTION: THE CLASSICAL ENGINEERING APPROACH

In the classical engineering fields the professional engineer designs machines, structures, systems, etc. which exhibit a high degree of reliability. Without these products and systems our society could not function in the way to which we have become accustomed. Examples of such engineering artefacts are buildings, roads, bridges, water and electric utilities, the telephone network, vehicles, ships, airplanes, chemical processing plants, etc. Many of these products and processes harbour great potential dangers and risks to property and life. We can, however, rely on these systems, for the engineers who design them are able to create plans free of a large class of potential errors. Most importantly, engineers are able to verify analytically, before actually building the object in question, that their design will satisfy the specifications.

A theoretical basis for designing error free programs has been developed during the last two decades. It is directly comparable to the theoretical foundations of the classical engineering fields and enables one to achieve similar results in terms of quality, reliability and freedom from design errors. It enables the software engineer to demonstrate, analytically and before running a proposed program, that it fulfills its specification – just as the civil engineer shows in his application for a construction permit that his proposed bridge design will support itself and the intended load.

It is not especially difficult to learn how to prove programs correct, but neither is it trivially simple. Learning this material and developing the ability to apply it in practice does take a certain amount of time, mental effort and the will to pursue a truly professional approach to software development. Software engineers experienced in its practical application report that this approach reduces the total software development time.

Where should one start to apply correctness proof methods? Software developers with pertinent experience agree that it is most productive and beneficial to utilize them already before and during the design phase, i.e. from the very beginning. This conclusion will not surprise the engineer, because the electrical engineer, for example, applies theoretical fundamentals when he conceives and designs his circuits, not only after he has completed his design. Similarly, the civil engineer employs his theoretical foundation (statics) during the design phase; he does not wait until he has completed the design or even until the stucture has been built.

If one starts to apply the correctness proof approach only after a program has been written, several difficulties can arise. Firstly, it may be impossible to prove the program correct simply because it is not correct. Secondly – if one succeeds in completing the proof – the proof may turn out to be unnecessarily logically complicated because the program itself is unnecessarily complicated. Thirdly, certain design decisions must be available in an appropriate form in order to complete the proof. Particularly important are loop invariants and pre- and postconditions for all called subprograms. If these design decisions are not available, then the corresponding design steps must be repeated when constructing the proof of correctness.

Frequently the attempt to prove a subprogram (or a program) correct leads to a new subprogram which is shorter and simpler than the original version and – in contrast to the original – correct.

By reducing the number of software errors – or even eliminating them completely – the costs of testing, finding and correcting errors can be substantially reduced and the productivity of the software development effort increased. Even more importantly, the reliability and quality of the delivered software will be substantially improved. Losses caused by software errors and the costs of repairing the damage will be reduced correspondingly.

It is not enough simply to write a program. Furthermore, it is not even enough to write a program which happens to be correct. We, like engineers in the classical disciplines, must also be able to convince ourselves and others that our design (program) is correct; we must explain why one can have confidence in our software. To paraphrase the French General Bosquet's famous comment on the battle of Balaclava, immortalized by Tennyson in "The Charge of the Light Brigade", what we software developers are now doing is magnificent, but it is not engineering.

1.3 INTENDED READERSHIP

This book is written for software developers working in industry or business and for those preparing for such positions.

It is conceived as a self-contained text for the practitioner who wants to write programs containing as few errors as possible without exploiting fully all possibilities of theoretical computing science and without having to learn the underlying theory completely.

For the professional software engineer and the software engineering student this book is intended as an *initial introduction* to the practical design of error free software and proving programs correct. After studying this book, readers in this group will want to complement their knowledge of the scientific and mathematical foundation of this field and to extend their ability to apply this material to other types of correctness statements (e.g. pre- and postconditions referring to data structures, pointer variables, etc.). (See [Baber, 1987].) Suggestions for such further study can be found in the Bibliography.

It is assumed that the reader is generally familiar with basic mathematics and has programming experience. If he is not yet able to manipulate algebraic (especially logical) expressions, he must be willing to acquire this ability during the course of studying this book. Appendix A gives a short introduction to this topic; many textbooks on computing contain more extensive sections on this subject.

In addition, the reader should be willing to examine critically his own prior experience and be open to new ideas and approaches to designing software. This book introduces him to a new software development world which is quite different from the one to which he is now accustomed.

1.4 GOALS OF THIS BOOK

The goals of this book are

- to familiarize the reader with the most important practically applicable aspects of proving computer programs correct,

- to show how these concepts can be used as a basis for writing error free programs,

- to enable the reader to apply these principles to actual design and programming tasks arising in his own daily work and

- to help the reader develop the ability to write demonstrably correct software himself.

After studying this book the reader will save time and effort and write significantly better software. His superior will rate him more highly and promote him before his more conservative colleagues. In the software world of tomorrow he will not be relegated to a position of unimportance.

It is the author's intention to present the material in this book in a simple, non-theoretical form. Theory cannot, of course, be avoided completely, but we will strive for an application oriented balance between theory and practice. In this book, practice takes precedence over theory.

1.5 CONTENTS OF THIS BOOK

In this book the emphasis is placed on the practical application of the material presented. A rigorous theoretical and mathematical foundation for this material exists but is not presented here. That theoretical foundation is mentioned only informally, and then only to the extent necessary to understand the proof rules and how to apply them.

This book deals only with logical assertions (preconditions, postconditions, etc.) which refer to the *values* of declared, active program variables. Such assertions are the most important which arise in practice and cover the main and most problematic aspects of program correctness. By restricting our attention to this type of assertion it is possible to minimize the time and effort required to learn this material while still covering most – but not quite all – proof techniques needed in professional software engineering practice. It is sometimes desirable or even necessary to include other types of assertions, e.g. about the structure of data environments, in specifications and proofs. Such needs arise, for example, in correctness proofs for recursive subprograms and calls thereto, where many variables with the same name but different values are maintained simultaneously in the data environment. Extensions of the approach described in this book to such other types of assertions can be found in the literature (see section 1.3 above and the Bibliography).

The metaphor in chapter 0, "The Sorcerer's Apprentices in the Land of the Ret Up Moc", expresses the notion that proving programs correct and designing error free software have a rational basis and constitute a professional approach to be taken seriously, despite the fact that some still consider them to be magic, unrealistic dreams or even charlatanry. Whether one likes it or not, they have a scientific basis and applying them responsibly is a professional engineering activity. In fact, their regular application in practice is an essential prerequisite for software *engineering* in the true sense of the word.

Chapter 1, "Introduction", discusses the background of the correctness proof approach, its practical application and its significance: the problem for society which software errors represent and the solution which our engineering predecessors developed long ago for comparable problems in other areas. Then the goals of this book are specified and its contents sketched.

Chapter 2, "The Execution of Program Statements: Effects and Assumptions", informally summarizes the definitions and assumptions upon which our program correctness proofs, proof rules and design guidelines are based.

Chapter 3, "Foundation for Correctness Proofs", begins with definitions of several key terms used frequently in the later sections. The very important, generally applicable proof rules are then introduced and explained. These proof rules form the basis of our practical work.

Chapter 4, "Analysis: Verifying the Correctness of a Program", explains and illustrates with many examples how to apply the proof rules in order to prove the correctness of a given program or subprogram. The correctness assertion about the program in question is decomposed into correctness assertions about smaller and smaller parts of the program until only assertions about individual assignment statements remain. The proof rules provide the basis for decomposing the various correctness assertions and for verifying the remaining assertions about assignment statements.

In chapter 5, "Designing a Correct Program", it is shown how the requirements of a correctness proof can serve as guidelines for designing a correct program and its parts. Such guidelines even make it possible to derive directly some parts of the program to be designed. This new approach, to which most programmers are not yet accustomed, leads systematically and straightforwardly to a compact, correct program. The program and its correctness proof are developed at the same time, with the proof tending to lead the way.

Chapter 6, "Formulating Pre- and Postconditions", discusses translating imprecise specifications in natural language into precise logical algebraic expressions (conditions).

Chapter 7, "Conclusion", summarizes the most important points and results of the preceding sections and previews briefly the engineering future of the field of software development.

Appendix A contains an introduction to logical (Boolean) algebra. The reader will use it to refresh his memory in certain areas and as a reference to look up specific details when needed.

Appendix B gives solutions to the exercises posed at various places in this book.

The Bibliography and the Index complete the book.

A reference card summarizing the practical application of the proof rules can be found inside the book.

2

THE EXECUTION OF PROGRAM STATEMENTS: EFFECTS AND ASSUMPTIONS

This chapter presents the assumptions about the effects of the various program statements upon which the proof rules introduced in chapter 3 and correctness proofs in general are based. These assumptions represent well known, but sometimes overlooked, characteristics of the statements.

The execution of a program statement has a specific effect, which depends in detail upon the particular characteristics of the programming language system in question. Typically, however, the general comments in the following sections apply.

Program statements of every type contain expressions. During the execution of a program statement, the value of every expression appearing therein is usually calculated. Therefore, we consider first the process of evaluating an expression.

2.1 THE EVALUATION OF EXPRESSIONS

When, during the execution of a program, an expression is to be evaluated, the following procedure is, in effect, carried out. First, each name of a program variable is replaced by the current value of the corresponding variable. Then the various operations appearing in the expression are executed. The result is the value of the expression.

Example: If the values of the variables x, y and z at the time in question are 3, 4 and 5 respectively, then the expression x*(y+z)<(x+z) will be evaluated as follows:

        x*(y+z) < (x+z)
        3*(4+5) < (3+5)
        3*9   < 8
        27   < 8
        false ∎

The value of an expression is, in general, defined only if the values of all variables occurring in the expression as well as all intermediate results calculated during the evaluation process are defined. In addition, all such values must lie within certain ranges. If these prerequisites are not satisfied, then the value of the expression is in general not defined; the execution of the program or compiler terminates with a corresponding error message.

Example: If the values of x, y and z are 3, "Henry" and 5 respectively, then the expression x*(y+z)<(x+z) will be evaluated as follows:

        x*(y+z)   < (x+z)
        3*("Henry"+5)   < (3+5)
        3*(not defined)   < 8
        not defined   < 8
        not defined ∎

The result of the addition (+) is not defined when one argument is a string (sequence of characters) such as "Henry". The undefined intermediate result propagates here through to the end of the evaluation process.

Some programming language systems, however, do permit undefined intermediate results in some circumstances and calculate well defined final results.

Example: Consider the array Y which is defined (declared) for the index values 1 through 10 inclusive only. Let the value of n be 11 and the value of x be 3. The expression (n≤10 **and** Y(n)=x) is to be evaluated:

> n≤10 **and** Y(n)=x
> 11≤10 **and** Y(11)=3
> false **and** (not defined=3)
> false **and** not defined
> false ■

One must pay careful attention to such implementational details. In the last example above, the system evaluates the expression (false **and** not defined) as false. Some systems, however, as in the previous example above, treat the value of this expression as not defined.

2.2 THE EXECUTION OF AN ASSIGNMENT STATEMENT

An assignment statement consists of the name of a variable, the assignment symbol (:=) and an expression, in which the names of any program variables may occur. The assignment statement is of the form:

> x:=E(x, y, ...)

When such an assignment statement is executed, the expression E(x, y, ...) is first evaluated (see section 2.1 above). Then the value of the expression is assigned to the variable x, i.e. becomes the new value of the variable x. The values of all other variables remain unchanged.

The result of executing an assignment statement is therefore defined if the variable x is declared (or will be automatically declared) and if the value of the expression E is defined and (after automatic conversion or rounding, if any) lies in the declared range of the variable x.

The effect of executing the above assignment statement can be summarized in the following axiom.

Axiom of the assignment statement: We write x' for the value of the variable x before the statement is executed, x" for the value after execution, etc. The values of the various variables before and after the execution of an assignment statement of the above form satisfy the following equations:

$$x" = E(x', y', ...)$$
$$y" = y', \text{ for all other variable names } y \blacksquare$$

Note the assumption that only the value of the variable whose name appears to the left of the assignment symbol (:=) is changed. So called "side effects", which change the values of other variables, are not permitted. If this assumption is violated, then neither the axiom of the assignment statement nor the proof rules following from it will, in general, be valid.

If the name of an array variable appears on the left side of an assignment statement, then the index expression is evaluated in order to determine the actual variable being referenced.

Example: If n=3, then the assignment statement

$$x(n):= ...$$

means

$$x(3):= ... \blacksquare$$

2.3 THE EXECUTION OF AN IF STATEMENT

The if statement is of the form

if B **then** S1 **else** S2 **endif**

where B is a condition (an expression whose value is either false or true) and S1 and S2 are statements. The names of any program variables may occur in the condition B. S1 and S2 may be compound statements, i.e. sequences of statements, if statements, loops, etc.

if-axiom: The execution of the if statement above has the same effect as the execution of

S1, if B'=true, or
S2, if B'=false $\blacksquare$

That is, the entire if statement is equivalent to either S1 or S2, depending upon whether B' is true or false.

B' is the value of the condition B before the if statement is executed. I.e., B' is determined by evaluating the condition B using the values of all pertinent variables immediately *before* execution of the if statement begins.

The result of executing an if statement is defined, therefore, if the value of the condition B is defined (false or true) and the result of executing S1 or S2 – depending upon the value of B – is defined.

The execution of an if statement
if B **then** S1 **else** S2 **endif**

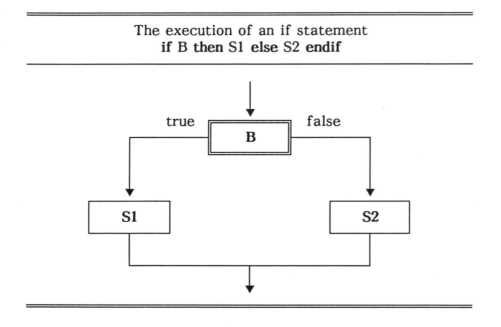

2.4 THE EXECUTION OF A SEQUENCE OF STATEMENTS

A sequence of statements is executed, as the name suggests, sequentially, one after the other. The result of the execution of the first statement in the sequence (i.e. the values of the program variables after the first statement has been executed) is the starting point for the execution of the second statement in the sequence, etc. Consequently, the result of the execution of the sequence of statements is defined if the execution of each individual statement in the sequence gives a defined result.

2.5 THE EXECUTION OF A WHILE LOOP

The while loop is of the form

while B **do** S **endwhile**

where B is a condition and S is a (possibly compound) statement.

while axiom: The execution of a while statement as the above has the same effect as the execution of

S
while B **do** S **endwhile**,   if B'=true, or

the empty statement,
i.e. nothing   if B'=false ∎

Thus, the first step of the execution of the while statement is to evaluate the condition B, based on the *previous* values of all pertinent variables. If this value is true, then S is executed and afterward the entire while statement is executed again. If the value of B is false, the entire while statement, including S, is skipped and succeeding statements (if any) in the program are executed.

If the value of the condition B is always true, then the loop body S is repeatedly executed and the loop never ends.

The result of executing a while loop is, therefore, defined if

* the value of the condition B is defined (false or true) every time it is evaluated and

* the result of every execution of the loop body S is defined and

* the value of the condition B is false after finitely many executions of the loop body S.

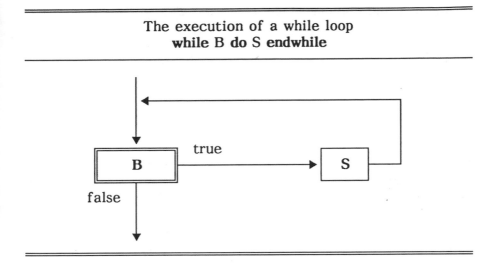

The execution of a while loop
while B do S endwhile

2.6 THE EXECUTION OF A SUBPROGRAM CALL

Executing a call to a subprogram without formal parameters has the same effect as executing the statements comprising the subprogram as if they had stood in place of the call statement.

Many programming languages permit passing parameters explicitly in the call to a subprogram. The mechanisms for passing parameters are implemented in different ways in different programming languages. When such parameter passing is to be taken into account in a correctness proof, it is usually easiest to translate (at least mentally) the call with formal parameter passing into an equivalent call without such parameters. The translated form of the call must correctly reflect the particular mechanisms for passing parameters in the target programming language. Then one proves the correctness of the resulting program containing only calls without formal parameter passing.

Example: Call   Called subprogram

             call U(x, y)   U(a, b):
                             result:=a+b

In many programming languages executing this call has the same effect as:

Call	Called subprogram
call U	U:
	a:=x
	b:=y
	result:=a+b

where a and b are variables which exist only inside the subprogram U. They are created when U is called and are released (deleted) when the execution of U terminates. ∎

3

FOUNDATION FOR CORRECTNESS PROOFS

In order to prove a program, a program segment or a statement correct, one formulates a mathematical theorem about the effect of executing the program segment in question. Then one proves the theorem. Such a theorem is almost always of the following form: If a particular condition is true immediately before the program segment is executed, then a (generally different) condition will be true after execution. Such conditions are called *preconditions* and *postconditions*.

Pre- and postconditions refer to program variables. Most, in fact, refer only to the *values* of program variables. In this book we will consider only pre- and postconditions of this type.

In order to simplify the proof, the correctness theorem as outlined above is divided into two parts. In one part, one shows that the program segment in question executes at all, i.e. that its execution terminates with a defined result (without a compilation or run time error). In the other part, one proves the correctness theorem mentioned above under the assumption that the program terminates.

3.1 DEFINITIONS

A *condition* is an algebraic expression whose value is "false" or "true". Typically names of program variables appear in an expression; each name stands for the value of the corresponding variable. Conditions are also called *logical* expressions, *Boolean* expressions and *assertions*.

Examples:

$x>8$
$y=4$
$x>3$ **and** $y+z>6$
CUSTOMERNAME="Smith"
$3000 \leq salary < 4000$
$A(1) \leq A(2) \leq \ldots \leq A(n)$
$A(1) \leq A(2)$ **and** $A(2) \leq A(3)$ **and** $\ldots A(n-1) \leq A(n)$

$$\textbf{and}_{i=1}^{n-1} A(i) \leq A(i+1) \blacksquare$$

If the truth of a condition V immediately before a program statement S is executed implies that a condition P is true afterward, then we say that V is a *precondition* of the *postcondition* P with respect to the statement S. Such a relationship between V, P and S is usually written $\{V\}$ S $\{P\}$. The statement S may be a single statement or a compound statement containing any number of individual statements, e.g. a program segment or a complete program.

Example: If $x>3$ before the assignment statement $x:=x+5$ is executed, then $x>8$ afterward. Symbolically,

$\{x>3\}$ $x:=x+5$ $\{x>8\}$ $\blacksquare$

The result of executing a statement, a program segment or a program is *correct* if it satisfies the given postcondition.

A program statement (or a program segment, program, etc.) *terminates* if its execution proceeds to the end in finite time

and without a run time error (and without a compilation error)
– i.e. if its execution yields a defined result.

If the execution of a statement, program segment or program yields a correct result whenever it terminates, then the
statement, etc. is said to be *partially* correct. If, in addition,
one has proved that it does terminate, then the statement, etc.
is said to be *totally* correct. Separating these two aspects of
correctness simplifies our proofs. Different approaches and
techniques are appropriate in these two parts of our proofs, as
we will see in chapter 4.

3.2 PRE- AND POSTCONDITIONS IN CORRECTNESS PROOFS

Pre- and postconditions are the key elements in a proof of
correctness. They represent the definition of "correctness" of a
particular program or program segment. Expressed differently,
a precondition and a postcondition together constitute the
specification of the program in question.

The essential parts of a typical proof of correctness deal
with pre- and postconditions and especially with the relationships between them. Sometimes one derives algebraically a
precondition for a given postcondition and a given program
statement (simple or compound). This approach is especially
useful for assignment statements. Often the task at hand is to
verify (prove) a correctness proposition about the pre- and
postconditions of a program segment. In this case, one first
decomposes the correctness proposition to be proved into
correctness propositions about component parts of the program
segment in question and then proves the latter. Several useful
rules, which are introduced in the following sections, facilitate
these steps.

3.3 PROOF RULES

In the following sections the most important generally applicable theorems needed in practice to prove programs correct are
presented in the form of "proof rules". For each program statement, simple or compound (assignment statement, if statement,

sequence of statements and while loop), one or more proof rules are presented and briefly explained. Additional proof rules enable one to simplify the algebraic manipulation of the logical expressions arising in a proof.

The subject of each proof rule is a relationship between a precondition and a postcondition. Analogies from other technical fields include Ohm's, Faraday's and Henry's laws (electrical engineering), each of which gives the relationship between voltage and current for a particular electrical component, and the equations for a mass, a spring and a viscous damper (mechanical engineering), each of which expresses the corresponding relationship between force and position.

We begin with a proof rule which sometimes enables us to simplify the algebraic manipulation of expressions arising in a proof. It follows from the definition of pre- and postconditions above and makes it easier to understand some of the other proof rules.

3.3.1 Proof rule P1: Strengthening a precondition and weakening a postcondition

If

$$V \implies V1 \text{ and}$$
$$\{V1\} \ S \ \{P1\} \text{ and}$$
$$P1 \implies P$$

then

$$\{V\} \ S \ \{P\} \ \blacksquare$$

Proof rule P1
(Strengthening a precondition, weakening a postcondition)

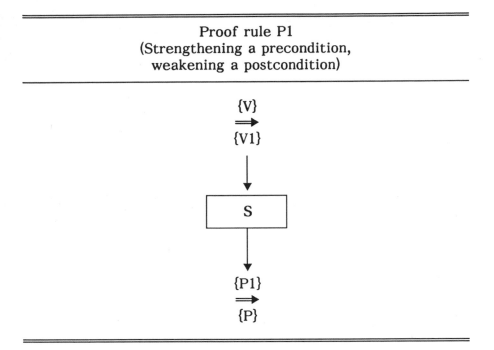

If the condition V is true before the statement S is executed and if V implies V1, then V1 is true before S is executed. If V1 is a precondition of P1 with respect to S, then P1 will be true after S is executed. If, finally, P1 implies P, then P will also be true after the execution of S. I.e., the truth of V before S is executed implies the truth of P afterward. Therefore, V is a precondition of P with respect to S (see the definition of a precondition in section 3.1 above).

Working *backwards* through a program, one may *strengthen* conditions. A condition can be strengthened by **and**ing an arbitrary term to it or by dropping an **or**ed term.

Working *forward* through a program, one may *weaken* conditions. A condition can be weakened by **or**ing an arbitrary term to it or by dropping an **and**ed term.

Judiciously strengthening preconditions and, less frequently, weakening postconditions can lead to simpler expressions and reduce (sometimes considerably) the amount of algebraic manipulation required to complete a proof. One must, however, be careful not to strengthen a precondition or weaken a postcondition so much that the proof cannot be completed. Later examples illustrate how this potential problem can be easily avoided.

3.3.2 Proof rule A1: Deriving a precondition of an assignment statement

To obtain a precondition of a given postcondition P with respect to a given assignment statement x:=E, substitute the expression (E) for every occurrence of the variable name x in the postcondition P. Symbolically,

$$\{P^x_E\} \; x:=E \; \{P\} \; \blacksquare$$

Proof rule A1 (Assignment statement)

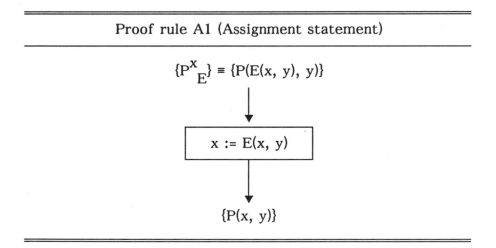

$$\{P^x_E\} \equiv \{P(E(x, y), y)\}$$

$$\boxed{x := E(x, y)}$$

$$\{P(x, y)\}$$

Do not forget to enclose the expression E in parentheses when substituting it for x in P. It is sometimes unnecessary, but never wrong to do so. It is sometimes wrong not to do so.

The value of x after executing the assignment statement x:=E is the same as the value of E before (see section 2.2). The value of y remains unchanged (assumption: no "side effects"). (The variable y here represents all program variables other than x.) Thus, the value of P(x, y) after executing the assignment statement is equal to the value of P(E, y) before. Therefore, the truth of P(E, y) before execution implies the truth of P(x, y) afterward and P(E, y) is a precondition of P(x, y) with respect to the assignment statement x:=E (see the definition of a precondition in section 3.1 above).

Example: In order to derive a precondition of the given post-condition {10<y **and** x<8} with respect to the assignment state-ment x:=x-5, we replace the variable x by the expression (x-5) in the given postcondition. The result is {10<y **and** (x-5)<8} or, equivalently, {10<y **and** x<13}. Symbolically,

$$\{10<y \textbf{ and } x<13\} \ x:=x-5 \ \{10<y \textbf{ and } x<8\}$$

By proof rule P1, every stronger condition is also a precondi-tion, e.g.

$$\{10<y \textbf{ and } 0 \le x<13\} \ x:=x-5 \ \{10<y \textbf{ and } x<8\}$$

and

$$\{10<y<x+N \textbf{ and } 0 \le x<13\} \ x:=x-5 \ \{10<y \textbf{ and } x<8\} \ \blacksquare$$

3.3.3 Proof rule A2: Verifying a precondition of an assignment statement

If

$$V \implies P^x_{\ E}$$

then

$$\{V\} \ x:=E \ \{P\} \ \blacksquare$$

Proof rule A2 (Assignment statement)

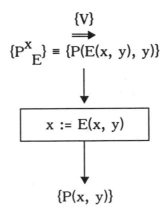

$$\{V\}$$
$$\Longrightarrow$$
$$\{P^x_E\} \equiv \{P(E(x, y), y)\}$$

$$x := E(x, y)$$

$$\{P(x, y)\}$$

Proof rule A2 is a combination of proof rules A1 and P1. By proof rule P1, V is a precondition of P with respect to the assignment statement if

$$(V \Longrightarrow P^x_E) \text{ and } \{P^x_E\} \text{ } x:= E \text{ } \{P\}$$

By proof rule A1,

$$\{P^x_E\} \text{ } x:=E \text{ } \{P\}$$

It suffices, therefore, to show that $V \Longrightarrow P^x_E$ when one wishes to verify that $\{V\}$ x:=E $\{P\}$.

When applying proof rule A2 one implicitly applies the two proof rules A1 and P1. In effect, proof rule A1 is used to derive a precondition. Then one verifies that the given precondition implies the derived precondition, i.e., that the hypothesis of proof rule P1 is satisfied.

3.3.4 Proof rule IF1: Verifying a precondition of an if statement

If

> {V and B} S1 {P} and
> {V and not B} S2 {P}

then

> {V} if B then S1 else S2 endif {P} ∎

Proof rule IF1 (if statement)

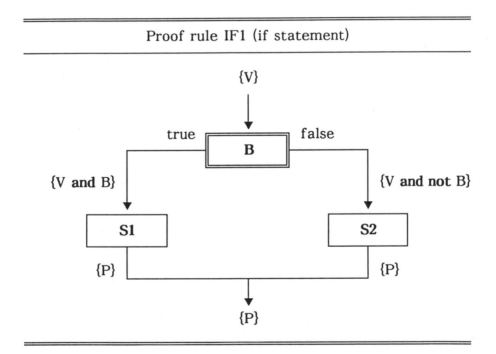

If the condition V is true before the if statement is executed, then both V and B will be true immediately before S1 is executed (if it is executed). Since (V and B) is a precondition of P with respect to S1, P will be true after execution of S1. Similarly, P will be true after the execution of S2. Thus, the truth of V before execution of the if statement implies in either case the truth of P afterward. Therefore, V is a precondition of P with respect to the entire if statement (see the definition in section 3.1).

3.3.5 Proof rule IF2: Deriving a precondition of an if statement

If

{V1} S1 {P} and
{V2} S2 {P}

then

{(V1 **and** B) **or** (V2 **and not** B)}
if B **then** S1 **else** S2 **endif** {P} ∎

Proof rule IF2 (if statement)

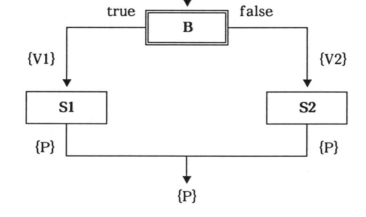

Proof rule IF2 is essentially proof rule IF1 with V = [(V1 **and** B) **or** (V2 **and not** B)]. Proof rule IF2 follows from proof rules IF1 and P1.

By applying proof rule IF2 one can derive a precondition of a given postcondition P with respect to a given if statement. First, derive preconditions of P with respect to the then and else parts S1 and S2, using the proof rules appropriate for those statements. Then combine the two preconditions in the manner shown above.

3.3.6 Proof rule IF3: If statement

If

$\qquad$ {V1} S1 {P} and
$\qquad$ {V2} S2 {P}

then

$\qquad$ {V1 and V2} if B then S1 else S2 endif {P} ∎

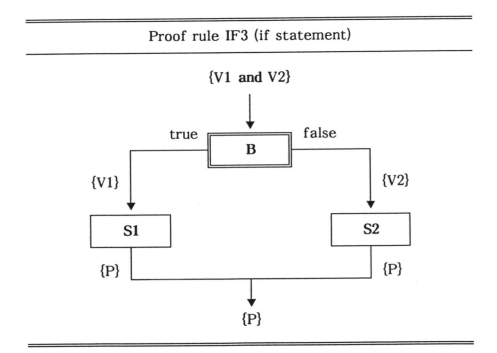

Proof rule IF3 (if statement)

Proof rule IF3 is a weak theorem, which follows from proof rules IF1 and P1. Because of the simple form of the expressions appearing in it, it is sometimes useful in practice.

3.3.7 Proof rule IF4: If statement

If

    {V1 **and** B} S1 {P} and
    {V2 **and not** B} S2 {P}

then

    {V1 **and** V2} **if** B **then** S1 **else** S2 **endif** {P} ∎

Proof rule IF4 (if statement)

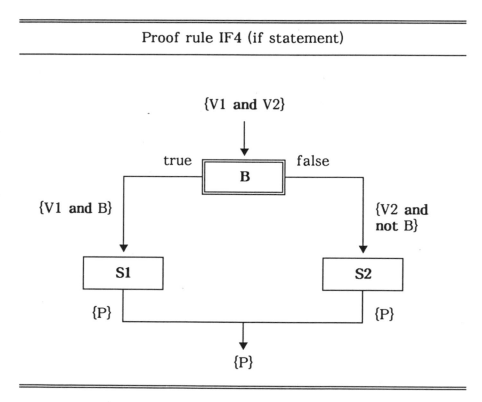

Proof rule IF4 also follows from proof rules IF1 and P1. Like proof rule IF3, it is sometimes of practical use because of the simple form of the precondition (V1 **and** V2).

3.3.8 Proof rule S1: Sequence of statements

If

> {V} S1 {P1} and
> {P1} S2 {P}

then

> {V} (S1; S2) {P} ∎

Proof rule S1 (Sequence of statements)

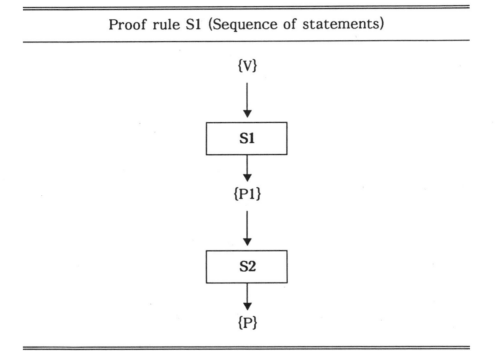

Proof rule S1 generalizes to an arbitrarily long sequence of statements in the obvious way. Thus, to find a precondition of a given postcondition P with respect to a sequence of statements, first find a precondition of P with respect to the last statement in the sequence. Then, use this as the postcondition with respect to the next to last statement, etc., working backward statement by statement through the entire sequence. The precondition with respect to the first statement in the sequence found in this way is also a precondition of P with respect to the entire sequence.

3.3.9 Proof rule W1: While loop without initialization

If

   {I **and** B} S {I}

then

   {I} **while** B **do** S **endwhile** {I **and not** B} ∎

Proof rule W1 (while loop)

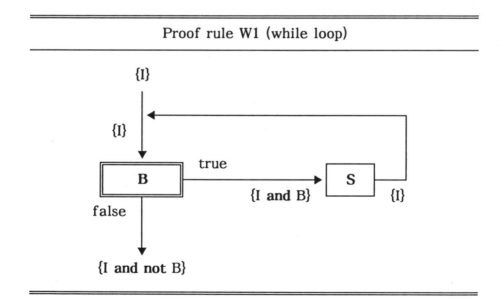

If the condition I is true immediately before execution of the while loop begins, then both I and B will be true before the first execution of the loop body S. Since (I **and** B) is a precondition of I with respect to S, I will be true after the first execution of S. Both I and B will, therefore, be true before the second execution of S, etc. The condition I will be true after every execution of S. If and when the execution of the loop comes to an end, I will be true and B will be false. I.e. the condition (I **and not** B) will be true when the loop terminates (if it terminates).

The value of the condition I is true, i.e. constant, before and after every execution of the loop body S. Therefore, the condition I is called the *loop invariant*. The loop invariant is the key to designing and to understanding a loop.

The application of proof rule W1 requires that the loop invariant I be true before the loop is executed. Typically, I is initially true in a trivial way. In other words, the initial situation is a special case of the loop invariant. When execution of the loop terminates, the condition (I **and not** B) is true. I.e., the final situation is also a special case of I. Viewed the other way around, the loop invariant I is a generalization of the initial and final situations. This observation suggests the very useful

Rule of thumb for determining a loop invariant: Generalize (weaken) the initial and final situations (the pre- and postconditions) in order to determine a suitable loop invariant. ∎

Preceding almost every loop is its "initialization", a program segment whose *only* purpose is to establish the initial truth of the loop invariant.

Very often one wishes to prove the correctness of a loop together with its initialization. For this purpose we have proof rule W2.

3.3.10 Proof rule W2: While loop with initialization

Let the condition I (the loop invariant) be given. If

> $\{V\}$ initialization $\{I\}$ and
> $\{I$ **and** $B\}$ S $\{I\}$ and
> $(I$ **and not** $B) \implies P$

then

> $\{V\}$ (initialization; **while** B **do** S **endwhile**) $\{P\}$ ∎

Proof rule W2 (while loop with initialization)

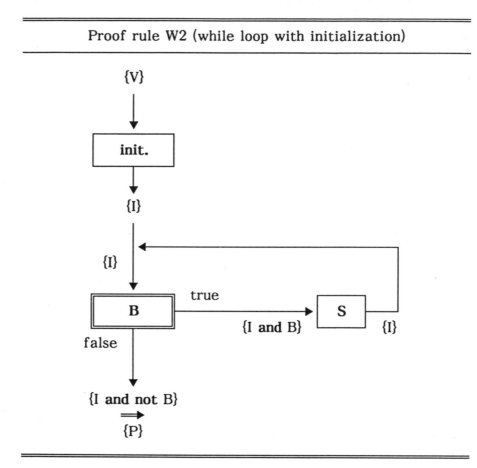

Proof rule W2 combines (and follows from) proof rules S1, P1 and W1.

To prove the partial correctness of a while loop by applying proof rule W2, one must

1. determine the loop invariant I (if not already given by the designer or programmer),
2. prove that {V} initialization {I} (i.e. that I is true initially),
3. prove that {I and B} S {I} (i.e., that the body of the loop preserves the truth of I) and
4. prove that (I and not B) $\Longrightarrow$ the postcondition P (i.e. that P is true on termination of the loop).

To prove that a loop is totally correct, one must in addition

5. show that the loop terminates, i.e. that there is an upper bound to the number of times S is executed (see section 2.5).

Termination is usually proved by showing that (1) the value of some expression is increased or decreased by at least a fixed amount by each execution of S and that (2) there is an upper or lower bound respectively on the value of that expression. Often the bound follows from the while condition B; sometimes it is part of the loop invariant. Such an expression is called a loop *variant*. Strictly speaking, step 5 also requires showing that the complete loop executes at all, i.e. that no "run time error" (e.g. overflow, reference to an undeclared variable, etc.) can occur.

3.3.11 Proof rule DC1: Divide and conquer

If

> {V1} S {P1} and
> {V2} S {P2}

then

> {V1 **and** V2} S {P1 **and** P2} ∎

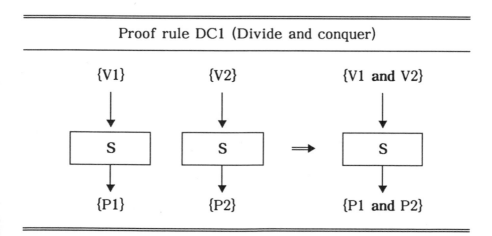

Proof rule DC1 (Divide and conquer)

Proof rule DC1 generalizes to an arbitrary number of terms (P1, P2, P3, P4, etc.) in the obvious way.

Sometimes a long expression arises in a correctness proof, for example, in the postcondition of a program segment. By applying proof rule DC1, one can split a long postcondition consisting of two or more **and**ed terms into shorter parts, derive the precondition for each part separately, and then recombine these preconditions. The total amount of effort is not reduced, but the proof is typically better organized, clearer and easier to understand. The individual steps in the algebraic manipulation are often much shorter and simpler. Even very long and complex expressions yield to the strategy "divide and conquer".

Proof rule DC1 applies to **and**ed terms. A comparable proof rule exists for **or**ed terms, too:

3.3.12 Proof rule DC2: Divide and conquer

If

   {V1} S {P1} and
   {V2} S {P2}

then

   {V1 **or** V2} S {P1 **or** P2} ∎

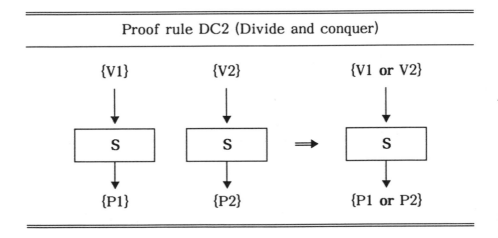

Proof rule DC2 (Divide and conquer)

3.3.13 Proof rule DC3: Divide and conquer

If

> {V} S {P1} and
> {V} S {P2}

then

> {V} S {P1 **and** P2} ∎

Proof rule DC3 (Divide and conquer)

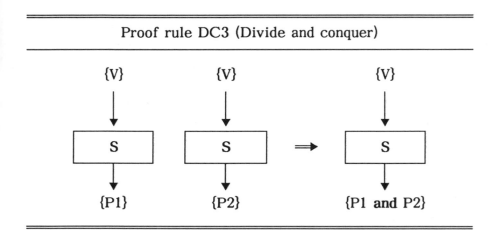

Proof rule DC3 is proof rule DC1 with V=V1=V2.

3.3.14 Proof rule DC4: Divide and conquer

If

> {V} S {P1} and
> {V} S {P2}

then

> {V} S {P1 **or** P2} ∎

Proof rule DC4 (Divide and conquer)

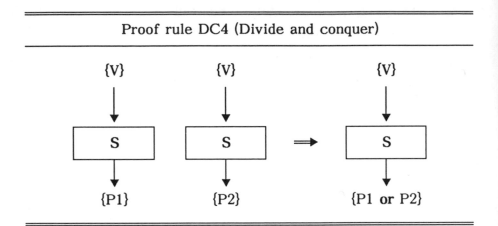

Proof rule DC4 is proof rule DC2 with V=V1=V2.

3.3.15 Proof rule SP1: Subprogram or program segment

If the values of all variables appearing in the condition B are left unchanged by the execution of a program segment S (e.g. a subprogram), then

$\{B\}$ S $\{B\}$ ∎

If in the condition B only variables appear whose values are the same before and after the execution of S, then the value of B before execution of S is clearly equal to the value of B afterward. Thus if B is true before, then B will be true afterward, and B is a precondition of itself with respect to S.

3.3.16 Proof rule SP2: Subprogram or program segment

If the values of all variables appearing in the condition B are left unchanged by the execution of a subprogram or program segment S and if

$\{V\}$ S $\{P\}$

then

$\{V$ **and** $B\}$ S $\{P$ **and** $B\}$

and

    {V or B} S {P or B} ∎

Proof rule SP2 follows from proof rules SP1, DC1 and DC2.

To apply proof rule SP2, separate the postcondition into two parts. One part should reference only variables whose values are not changed by the execution of S. This part of the postcondition is (by proof rule SP1) its own precondition. The second part of the postcondition contains all references to variables whose values are (or may possibly be) changed by the execution of S; derive a precondition of this part of the postcondition (e.g. by applying the appropriate proof rules or by referring to the formal specification of S). Finally, combine these two partial preconditions to form the desired precondition.

3.3.17 Proof rule SP3: Subprogram or program segment

If the values of all variables appearing in the condition B are left unchanged by the execution of a subprogram or program segment S and if

    $V \implies V1$ and
    {V1} S {P1} and
    $P1 \implies P$

then

    {V and B} S {P and B}

and

    {V or B} S {P or B} ∎

Proof rule SP3 is a combination of proof rules SP2 and P1.

That part of the postcondition which depends upon the effect of executing S (i.e. P above) may be weaker than the postcondition actually established by executing S (i.e. P1). Similarly, the relevant part of the precondition actually satisfied before executing S (i.e. V) may be stronger than the precondition required for the satisfactory functioning of S (i.e. V1).

3.4 APPLYING THE PROOF RULES

In order to prove a program or program segment correct, the meaning of "correct" with respect to the particular program in question must be explicitly defined. At least the postcondition must be known. Often the precondition is also given, in which case one must prove the given correctness proposition, i.e. verify that the given precondition is, in fact, a precondition of the given postcondition with respect to the given program. In other cases a precondition is to be derived for a given postcondition and a given program.

The choice of the appropriate proof rule to apply depends upon (1) the type of program statement in question and (2) whether a precondition is given or is to be derived. The following table can be used to select the proof rule(s) applicable in each case.

Proof rules DC1 through DC4 can be applied to all types of statements and to both proof tasks (verifying and deriving a precondition) in order to decompose lengthy conditions into smaller subexpressions.

A reference card for applying the proof rules is enclosed with this book. It can be used first to select the appropriate proof rule(s) for the task at hand. In addition, the card concisely explains the practical application of the proof rules. The reference card will be especially helpful as a memory aid to the reader who has learned the proof rules but has not yet become experienced in their use.

Selecting the appropriate proof rule(s)		
Statement type	Precondition	Proof rule(s)
assignment	given	A2
	to be derived	A1
if	given	IF1 (in some cases IF3 or IF4)
	to be derived	IF2
sequence	given	S1 (+ P1)
	to be derived	S1
while loop with initialization	given	W2
	to be derived	W2
while loop without initialization	given	W1 (+ P1)
	to be derived	W1
subprogram or program segment	given	SP2 (or SP3)
	to be derived	SP2 (or SP3)

3.5 IMPLICATIONS FOR PROGRAM DOCUMENTATION

Several requirements which the documentation of a program must satisfy derive from the proof rules and their practical application in proving programs correct.

First and foremost, pre- and postconditions must be included in the documentation. They must be formulated as logical algebraic expressions. These formulas should be supplemented by brief explanations in natural language and diagrams as appropriate to help the reader understand them as quickly and as easily as possible. See the examples in sections 4.4.1, 4.4.2, 4.5, 5.1.1, 5.2, 5.3.2 and 5.4.2.

The documentation of a subprogram should unambiguously indicate which variables are not affected by its execution. Usually this requirement is satisfied by listing *all* variables which are (or, more precisely, can be) modified by the subprogram in question. This information is a prerequisite for applying proof rules SP1, SP2 and SP3 (see sections 3.3.15-17, cf. the condition B appearing therein).

Absolutely essential in the documentation is a loop invariant for *every* loop.

In addition, conditions (assertions) which must be true at selected places in the subprogram should be given in the documentation. Particularly appropriate in this regard are places between loops and if statements as well as before and after a sequence of assignment statements. Conditions which can be derived easily and directly from other conditions in the documentation need not be included. Conditions which represent design decisions or which can be derived only by lengthy, time consuming algebraic manipulation should be included in the documentation.

The conditions to be included in the documentation as stated above are particularly useful when proving the correctness of the program later and when "maintaining" (modifying) it.

Every programmer who writes a call to the subprogram being documented must know its pre- and postconditions and which variables its execution can modify. The precondition tells him what state his program must establish before calling the subprogram, i.e. what he must be concerned with before the call. The postcondition tells him what he may assume to be true after the call.

4

ANALYSIS: VERIFYING THE CORRECTNESS OF A PROGRAM

In the process of proving a program segment or an entire program correct, one almost always needs either

- to verify that a given precondition is, in fact, a precondition of the given postcondition with respect to the given program or
- to derive a precondition of the given postcondition with respect to the given program.

In either case it is usually best to decompose the task in question in a way corresponding to the program's structure by applying the appropriate proof rules (see the table in section 3.4). Following this approach, one starts with the overall program structure and works iteratively inward to smaller program segments until only proof tasks involving individual assignment statements remain. Finally, these are solved by applying proof rules A1 and A2 for assignment statements.

For didactical reasons we will examine the proof process in the opposite order in this chapter. We will begin with the simplest, smallest program segments – individual assignment statements – and then extend our knowledge to the if statement, short sequences of statements and, finally, longer sequences involving a while loop with its initialization.

4.1 THE ASSIGNMENT STATEMENT

Proof rules A1 and A2 are used to prove the correctness of assignment statements. If a precondition is to be derived, we apply proof rule A1. If a given precondition is to be verified, we apply proof rule A2. (See sections 3.3.2 and 3.3.3.)

Proof rules A1 and A2 are applicable to assignments both to a simple variable and to an array (subscripted, indexed) variable. In proofs for assignments to an indexed variable one must, however, pay careful attention to certain details; therefore, a separate section (4.1.3) is devoted to this topic.

4.1.1 Assignment to a simple variable

The application of proof rules A1 and A2 is probably most easily explained and understood by studying some examples.

Example: A precondition is to be derived for the following assignment statement and postcondition:

$\{?\}$ x:=z-y $\{x-y>0\}$

Because our task is to derive a precondition with respect to an assignment statement, we apply proof rule A1 (see the table in section 3.4 and the reference card). According to proof rule A1, we must substitute the expression (z-y) for every occurrence of the variable x in the postcondition in order to obtain the precondition:

$\{x-y>0\}$ [postcondition]
$\{(z-y)-y>0\}$ [precondition]
$\{z-2*y>0\}$ [precondition]

Thus we have determined that

   {z−2*y>0} x:=z−y {x−y>0} ■

The parentheses around the expression (z−y) were superfluous in the above example. Sometimes, however, they are necessary, as the following example illustrates.

Example: Determine a precondition:

   {?} x:=z−y {y−x>0}

Applying proof rule A1, we substitute the expression (z−y) for x in the postcondition:

{y−x>0}	[postcondition]
{y−(z−y)>0}	[precondition]
{y−z+y>0}	[precondition]
{2*y−z>0}	[precondition]

That is,

   {2*y−z>0} x:=z−y {y−x>0} ■

To verify a given precondition for a given postcondition and assignment statement, one applies proof rule A2. In effect, one first derives a precondition. Then, one verifies that the given precondition implies the derived precondition.

Example: The correctness proposition

   {10<y<x+N and 0≤x<13} x:=x−5 {10<y and x<8}

is to be verified. At this point we note that the notational form a≤b≤c is nothing other than an abbreviation for (a≤b and b≤c). The above proposition has, therefore, the same meaning as

   {10<y and y<x+N and 0≤x and x<13} x:=x−5 {10<y and x<8}

According to proof rule A2 the above proposition will be true if

   {10<y and y<x+N and 0≤x and x<13}

   $\implies$ {10<y and x<8}$^{x}_{x-5}$

I.e., we must show that

   {10<y and y<x+N and 0≤x and x<13} $\implies$ {10<y and x−5<8} or, equivalently, that

$$\{10<y \text{ and } y<x+N \text{ and } 0\leq x \text{ and } x<13\} \implies \{10<y \text{ and } x<13\}$$

It can be easily seen that the given precondition (the left part of the above implication) is stronger than the derived precondition (the right part of the above implication) – i.e., that the above implication is true. (See Appendix A, section A.4, exercise 2.) The correctness proposition to be verified is, therefore, true by proof rule A2. ■

Exercise: Solve the following problems.

1. $\{?\}$ i:=i+1 $\{1\leq i\}$
2. $\{?\}$ sum:=sum+z $\{sum=x+y+z\}$
3. $\{?\}$ x:=5-z $\{w*y - 2*w^2 < z\}$ ■

4.1.2 What if it doesn't work?

(This section deals with advanced aspects of correctness proofs for assignment statements and may be skipped on first reading.)

The approach introduced and described in section 4.1.1 above is generally applicable to assignment statements. If, however, an attempt to prove the correctness of an assignment statement using that approach (i.e., by showing that the given precondition implies the derived precondition) is unsuccessful, then one of the following two situations must apply. Either

• the logical expressions have not yet been reformulated (manipulated) appropriately to complete the proof or

• the given, supposed precondition is not, in fact, a precondition of the given postcondition with respect to the given assignment statement, i.e. the program segment in question contains one or more errors.

The latter possibility must always be seriously considered, for many a program whose correctness is to be demonstrated is not, in fact, correct, but rather does contain errors.

When the proof cannot be successfully completed, one should try to find values for the program variables which fulfill the given, supposed precondition but not the derived precondition.

Such a set of values constitutes a test case which will demon-strate the presence of an error in the program.

An attempt to prove an erroneous program correct often leads directly to the location of the error in the program and even to a correction of the error.

Example: This example is an extract of an erroneous subpro-gram for merging the elements of two sorted arrays. The proof task is to show that

$\{ia \leq na+1$ **and** $(ia \leq na$ **and** $ib > nb$
          or $ia \leq na$ **and** $A(ia) \leq B(ib)$
          or $ib \leq nb$ **and** $A(ia) \leq B(ib))\}$
$ia := ia+1$ $\{ia \leq na+1\}$

(which is, however, not true).

According to proof rule A2, this correctness proposition will be true if

$\{ia \leq na+1$ **and** $(ia \leq na$ **and** $ib > nb$
          or $ia \leq na$ **and** $A(ia) \leq B(ib)$
          or $ib \leq nb$ **and** $A(ia) \leq B(ib))\}$

$\implies \{ia \leq na+1\}^{ia}_{ia+1}$

or, equivalently,

$\{ia \leq na+1$ **and** $(ia \leq na$ **and** $ib > nb$
          or $ia \leq na$ **and** $A(ia) \leq B(ib)$
          or $ib \leq nb$ **and** $A(ia) \leq B(ib))\}$

$\implies \{ia \leq na\}$

The derived precondition $\{ia \leq na\}$ does not follow from the given precondition (the left part of the implication above). We raise, therefore, the question, under what circumstances is the given precondition fulfilled (i.e. true), but the derived precondi-tion not (i.e. false)? The negation of the derived precondition is $ia > na$. If the given precondition is to be fulfilled, but the de-rived precondition not, then $ia = na+1$. The first two **or**ed terms above will then be false; the other must, therefore, be true. Consequently, our test case (counterexample refuting the program's correctness) must satisfy the following conditions:

    ia=na+1
    ib≤nb
    A(ia)≤B(ib)

The lack of the condition ia≤na in the third ored term of the given precondition prevents us from completing our correctness proof. This term comes from an if condition in the subprogram from which this example was taken. The correction of the error follows already from our analysis: the condition ia≤na must be anded to the if condition referred to above. ∎

4.1.3 Assignment to an indexed (array) variable

(This section deals with advanced aspects of correctness proofs for assignment statements and may be skipped on first reading.)

An assignment statement which assigns a new value to an array variable is, in principle, handled exactly as described in section 4.1.1. One must, however, pay particularly careful attention to the question of which references in the postcondition to an array variable should be replaced by the appropriate expression and which should not. The following example illustrates the potentially problematic nature of this question.

Example: A precondition is to be derived:

    {?} y(m):=z {y(m)=y(n)}

Clearly, "y(m)" in the postcondition should be replaced by "(z)" in accordance with proof rule A1. In addition, it must be noted that the execution of this assignment statement can, under certain circumstances, change the value of y(n) also, namely when the values of m and n are equal and "y(m)" and "y(n)" therefore refer to the *same* array variable. In this case, also "y(n)" must be replaced by "(z)"; otherwise, not.

If m=n, then the desired precondition is {z=z} or simply the logical constant true. If m≠n, then the desired precondition is {z=y(n)}. In other words, the precondition V is

    V = true,   if m=n
      = [z=y(n)],   if m≠n

Another expression for the same condition V is (see Appendix A, section A.4, exercise 1 and its solution in Appendix B):

$$V$$
$$=$$
$$[(m=n) \text{ and true or } (m\neq n) \text{ and } z=y(n)]$$
$$=$$
$$[m=n \text{ or } z=y(n)]$$

(See Appendix A, section A.3, identities 10 and 17.) ∎

By reformulating the postcondition appropriately, references to array variables can frequently be separated so that certain references must always be replaced and the others, never. Especially when **and** and **or** series occur in the postcondition should one look for this possibility.

Example: After the execution of the assignment statement $D(j):=A(k)$, we require that the array variables $D(1)$ through $D(j)$ be sorted, i.e. $D(1) \leq D(2) \ldots \leq D(j)$. The precondition which ensures that this will be the case is to be derived:

$$\{?\} \; D(j):=A(k) \; \{\text{and}_{i=1}^{j-1} \; D(i) \leq D(i+1)\}$$

Inside the **and** series the value of the running variable i is always less than j, i.e. $i \neq j$. Thus, $D(i)$ never refers to $D(j)$ and, hence, is not to be replaced by "A(k)". The variable $D(i+1)$ refers to $D(j)$ when $i=j-1$, otherwise not. This observation suggests taking the one term out of the **and** series (see Appendix A, section A.5). Accordingly, we rewrite our proof task as follows:

$$\{?\} \; D(j):=A(k)$$
$$\{j<2 \text{ or } j\geq2 \text{ and } D(j-1)\leq D(j) \text{ and}_{i=1}^{j-2} \; D(i)\leq D(i+1)\}$$

Expressed in this form, the postcondition contains exactly one reference to $D(j)$. The values of the index expressions in all other references to array variables $D(.)$ are less than – and hence different from – the value of j. The desired precondition can now be derived by substituting $A(k)$ for the one occurrence of $D(j)$ in the last expression for the postcondition above:

$$\{j<2 \text{ or } j\geq2 \text{ and } D(j-1)\leq A(k) \text{ and}_{i=1}^{j-2} \; D(i)\leq D(i+1)\} \; ∎$$

This precondition requires that either

- the array D is empty (j<2) or

- the value of A(k) is at least as great as the value of the last element of the array D and the elements already in D are sorted (whereby an array containing only one element (j=2) is sorted).

A detailed discussion of dealing with assignments to array variables in correctness proofs as well as a generally applicable solution to this problem can be found in [Baber, 1987, pp. 72, 73 and 140 ff.].

4.2 THE IF STATEMENT

For the if statement we have several proof rules among which to choose. The most important of these are IF1 and IF2. The others, IF3 and IF4, are weaker versions of IF1. Only because of the simpler forms of the logical expressions appearing in them are they sometimes of practical interest. (See sections 3.3.4 through 3.3.7.)

When a precondition is to be derived for a given postcondition and if statement, proof rule IF2 is used. Its application effectively decomposes the proof task in question into subtasks reflecting the structure of the if statement. The preconditions with respect to the then and else parts of the if statement are derived and then combined as specified by proof rule IF2. The result is the desired precondition with respect to the entire if statement.

When a given precondition of a given postcondition and if statement is to be verified, proof rule IF1 is usually used. If the given expressions match the form of proof rule IF3 or IF4, then it may be applied instead of proof rule IF1. In any case the correctness proposition about the entire if statement is decomposed into two subsidiary correctness propositions: one about the then part of the if statement and the other about the else part. The resulting correctness propositions must then be verified in turn by applying the appropriate proof rules.

Example 1: A precondition is to be derived for the following postcondition and if statement.

$\{?\}$ **if** $x<0$ **then** $y:=-x$ **else** $y:=x$ **endif** $\{y>0\}$

Proof rule IF2 is appropriate for this task (see the table in section 3.4 and the reference card). It decomposes by proof rule IF2 into three subtasks: Derive V1 and V2 such that

$\{V1?\}$ $y:=-x$ $\{y>0\}$ and
$\{V2?\}$ $y:=x$ $\{y>0\}$

and form (and simplify, if possible) the expression

$\{(V1$ **and** $x<0)$ **or** $(V2$ **and not** $x<0)\}$

which is the desired precondition V.

V1, a precondition with respect to an assignment statement, is to be derived; we must, therefore, apply proof rule A1. Replacing the variable y by the expression $(-x)$ in the postcondition, we obtain the precondition

V1

$=$

$\{y>0\}^y_{(-x)}$

$=$

$\{(-x)>0\}$

$=$

$\{x<0\}$

In order to derive V2, we replace the variable y by the expression (x) in the postcondition and obtain the precondition

V2

$=$

$\{y>0\}^y_x$

$=$

$\{x>0\}$

Finally we combine V1 and V2 as specified by proof rule IF2 to form the desired precondition V with respect to the entire if statement:

V
=
{(V1 **and** x<0) **or** (V2 **and not** x<0)}
=
{(x<0 **and** x<0) **or** (x>0 **and** x≥0)}

This expression for V can be simplified (see Appendix A, section A.3):

V
=
{(x<0) **or** (x>0)}
=
{x≠0} ∎

Example 1:
Deriving a precondition for an if statement

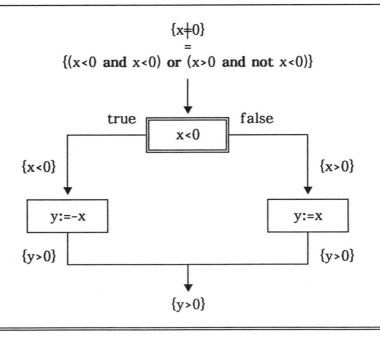

{x≠0}
=
{(x<0 **and** x<0) **or** (x>0 **and not** x<0)}

true   false
x<0

{x<0}   {x>0}

y:=-x   y:=x

{y>0}   {y>0}

{y>0}

The following, somewhat more complex example can be solved in essentially the same way.

Example 2: A precondition is to be derived:

{?} **if** x<0 **then** y:=x **else** y:=x-2 **endif** {-1≤y≤4}

By applying proof rule IF2 we decompose this task into three subtasks:

{V1?} y:=x {-1≤y≤4}
{V2?} y:=x-2 {-1≤y≤4}
V = {(V1 **and** x<0) **or** (V2 **and not** x<0)}

By applying proof rule A1 we derive the precondition V1:

V1

=

{-1≤y≤4}^y_x

=

{-1≤x≤4}

and the precondition V2:

V2

=

{-1≤y≤4}^{y}(x-2)

=

{-1≤(x-2)≤4}

=

{1≤x≤6}

Substituting these expressions for V1 and V2 in the expression for V above, we obtain for the desired precondition

V

=

{(-1≤x≤4 **and** x<0) **or** (1≤x≤6 **and** x≥0)}

=

{-1≤x<0 **or** 1≤x≤6} ∎

Example 2:
Deriving a precondition for an if statement

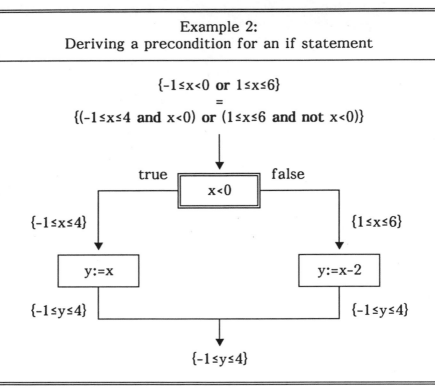

{-1≤x<0 **or** 1≤x≤6}
=
{(-1≤x≤4 **and** x<0) **or** (1≤x≤6 **and** **not** x<0)}

true   x<0   false

{-1≤x≤4}   {1≤x≤6}

y:=x   y:=x-2

{-1≤y≤4}   {-1≤y≤4}

{-1≤y≤4}

Example 3: The correctness proposition

> {ia≤na **or** ia≤na+1 **and** ib≤nb}
> **if** ib>nb **or** ia≤na **then** ia:=ia+1 **else** ib:=ib+1 **endif**
> {ia≤na+1}

is to be verified, i.e. the precondition given above is to be verified.

According to proof rule IF1, this correctness proposition will be true if the following two correctness propositions are true:

> {(ia≤na **or** ia≤na+1 **and** ib≤nb)   [Proposition 1]
> **and** (ib>nb **or** ia≤na)}
> ia:=ia+1 {ia≤na+1}

> {(ia≤na **or** ia≤na+1 **and** ib≤nb)   [Proposition 2]
> **and** **not** (ib>nb **or** ia≤na)}
> ib:=ib+1 {ia≤na+1}

By applying proof rule IF1 we have decomposed the original proof task of verifying the correctness of an entire if statement into two subtasks, each of which involves verifying the correctness of a single assignment statement.

Proposition 1: By proof rule A2, proposition 1 above will be true if

$\{($ia$\leq$na **or** ia$\leq$na+1 **and** ib$\leq$nb$)$ **and** $($ib$>$nb **or** ia$\leq$na$)\}$
$\Longrightarrow \{$ia$\leq$na$\}$

Simplifying the left expression in the above implication, we obtain (see Appendix A, section A.3):

$\{($ia$\leq$na **or** ia$\leq$na+1 **and** ib$\leq$nb$)$
and $($ib$>$nb **or** ia$\leq$na$)\}$

=

$\{$ia$\leq$na **and** ib$>$nb
or ia$\leq$na **and** ia$\leq$na
or ia$\leq$na+1 **and** ib$\leq$nb **and** ib$>$nb
or ia$\leq$na+1 **and** ib$\leq$nb **and** ia$\leq$na$\}$

=

$\{$ia$\leq$na **and** ib$>$nb
or ia$\leq$na
or false
or ia$\leq$na **and** ib$\leq$nb$\}$

=

$\{$ia$\leq$na$\}$

Thus, proposition 1 reduces to $[\{$ia$\leq$na$\} \Longrightarrow \{$ia$\leq$na$\}]$, which is obviously true.

Proposition 2: By proof rule A2, proposition 2 above will be true if

$\{($ia$\leq$na **or** ia$\leq$na+1 **and** ib$\leq$nb$)$
and not $($ib$>$nb **or** ia$\leq$na$)\}$
$\Longrightarrow \{$ia$\leq$na+1$\}$

It is evident that the right condition in the implication above $\{$ia$\leq$na+1$\}$ follows from the first **and**ed subexpression in the left part of the implication. Formally (see Appendix A, section A.3 and section A.4, exercise 2),

{(ia≤na **or** ia≤na+1 **and** ib≤nb)
and not (ib>nb **or** ia≤na)}

=

{(ia≤na **or** ia≤na+1 **and** ib≤nb) **and** ...}

⟹

{ia≤na **or** ia≤na+1 **and** ib≤nb}

⟹

{ia≤na **or** ia≤na+1 **and** ib≤nb **or** ia≤na+1}

=

{ia≤na+1} ∎

Example 3:
Verifying the correctness of an if statement

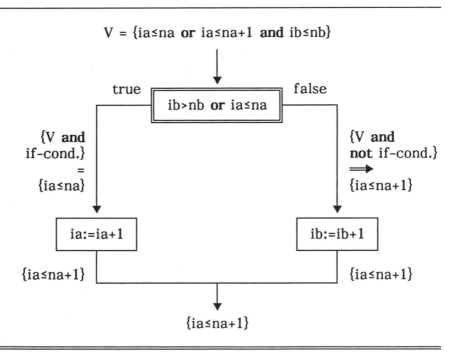

V = {ia≤na **or** ia≤na+1 **and** ib≤nb}

true   ib>nb **or** ia≤na   false

{V **and** if-cond.} = {ia≤na}

{V **and** **not** if-cond.} ⟹ {ia≤na+1}

ia:=ia+1   ib:=ib+1

{ia≤na+1}   {ia≤na+1}

{ia≤na+1}

Exercise: Solve the following problems.

1. {?} **if** x<0 **then** y:=-x **else** y:=x **endif** {y>0}
2. {?} **if** x<0 **then** y:=-x **else** y:=x **endif** {y≥0}
3. {?} **if** x<0 **then** y:=-x **else** y:=x **endif** {y<0}

4. $\{?\}$ **if** x<0 **then** y:=-x **else** y:=x **endif** $\{y \le 0\}$
5. $\{3 \le |x| \le 4\}$ **if** x<0 **then** y:=-x **else** y:=x **endif** $\{2 \le y \le 4\}$? ∎

4.3 THE SEQUENCE OF STATEMENTS

The correctness of a sequence of statements is proved by applying proof rule S1 (see section 3.3.8). One begins with the postcondition and, working backward through the sequence of statements, derives a precondition for each statement. The precondition with respect to the first statement in the sequence derived in this way is also a precondition with respect to the entire sequence.

Example: A precondition is to be derived for the following postcondition and sequence of statements:

$\{V?\}$ gr:=gr-1; gl:=gl-1 $\{il-1 \le gl < gr \le ig\}$

Applying proof rule S1, we decompose this proof task into two subtasks, each involving a single assignment statement:

$\{V?\}$ gr:=gr-1 $\{P1\}$ [P1 still to be determined]

and

$\{P1?\}$ gl:=gl-1 $\{il-1 \le gl < gr \le ig\}$

Because P1 is unknown, we cannot yet solve the subtask for the first assignment statement. We must start with the last one. We derive P1 by applying proof rule A1, substituting the expression (gl-1) for the variable gl in the postcondition:

P1 = $\{il-1 \le gl-1 < gr \le ig\}$

The subtask for the first assignment statement then becomes

$\{V?\}$ gr:=gr-1 $\{il-1 \le gl-1 < gr \le ig\}$

Applying proof rule A1, we substitute the expression (gr-1) for the variable gr in P1 (which is now the postcondition of the first assignment statement in the sequence) in order to derive the desired precondition.

V = $\{il-1 \le gl-1 < gr-1 \le ig\}$

Summarizing (and repeating), we have shown that

$\{il-1 \le gl-1 < gr-1 \le ig\}$ gr:=gr-1 $\{il-1 \le gl-1 < gr \le ig\}$

and

$\{il-1 \le gl-1 < gr \le ig\}$ gl:=gl-1 $\{il-1 \le gl < gr \le ig\}$

from which it follows by proof rule S1 that

$\{il-1 \le gl-1 < gr-1 \le ig\}$ gr:=gr-1; gl:=gl-1 $\{il-1 \le gl < gr \le ig\}$ ∎

Exercise: Show that the following correctness proposition about the given sequence of statements is true.

1. $\{0 \le N\}$ i:=0; j:=0

$\{\text{and}_{k=0}^{j-1} \ (\text{not and}_{a=0}^{N-1} \ D(k+a)=K(a))$

and $(j>M-N \text{ or } j \le M-N \ \text{and}_{a=0}^{i-1} \ D(j+a)=K(a))$

and $0 \le j$ and $0 \le i \le N\}$ ∎

4.4 THE WHILE LOOP

Proof rules W1 and W2 are used to prove the correctness of a while loop, depending upon whether the proof task involves a loop without or with initialization respectively. Most often the subject of the proof task is a loop with initialization. Therefore, we will devote our attention here to proof rule W2, which includes proof rule W1 as a component part anyway. (See sections 3.3.9 and 3.3.10.)

By applying proof rule W2, one decomposes the task of proving the correctness of a loop with initialization into three subtasks: proving (1) the correctness of the initialization, (2) the correctness of the loop body and (3) the truth of the post-condition upon termination of the loop. Each of these subtasks is solved by applying the appropriate proof rule(s) or by suitably transforming the logical algebraic expressions in question.

Finally one must show that the loop will terminate, especially that the body of the loop will be executed only a limited number of times.

A suitable loop invariant must be known before proof rule W2 can be applied. Determining the loop invariant is actually a design decision. The loop invariant should, therefore, be stated explicitly in the documentation on the program in which the loop appears. Because its inclusion in the documentation cannot yet be taken for granted, however, this design step must sometimes be repeated before a formal correctness proof can be completed.

In section 4.4.1 below we will prove the correctness of a while loop for which a loop invariant is known. In section 4.4.2 we will see how to determine a suitable loop invariant when none is given.

4.4.1 Correctness proof (loop invariant known)

Example: Prove the correctness of the following subprogram, which searches the array A for the value of the variable x.

```
k:=1
while k≤n and A(k)≠x do k:=k+1 endwhile
```

The specified precondition is

$n \epsilon Z$ **and** $0 \le n$

where Z is the set of all integers (0, 1, -1, 2, -2, ...). I.e. the phrase "$n \epsilon Z$" means "the value of the variable n is an integer".

The variable n indicates how many elements the array A contains.

The given postcondition is

$n \epsilon Z$ **and** $k \epsilon Z$ **and** $1 \le k \le n+1$ [range of k]

and $\prod_{i=1}^{k-1} A(i) \ne x$ [all elements before the k-th $\ne$ x]

and ($k \le n$ **and** $A(k)=x$ [A(k) = x]

    or $k=n+1$)   [no element of A = x]

The correctness proposition to be proved is, therefore,

$\{n\epsilon Z \text{ and } 0 \le n\}$
k:=1
while $k \le n$ **and** $A(k) \neq x$ **do** k:=k+1 **endwhile**

$\{n\epsilon Z \text{ and } k\epsilon Z \text{ and } 1 \le k \le n+1 \text{ and }_{i=1}{}^{k-1} A(i) \neq x$

and $(k \le n$ **and** $A(k)=x$ **or** $k=n+1)\}$

The programmer specified the loop invariant I to be as follows:

$n\epsilon Z$ **and** $k\epsilon Z$ **and** $1 \le k \le n+1$ [range of k]

and$_{i=1}{}^{k-1} A(i) \neq x$ [all elements before the k-th $\neq$ x]

Because the correctness proposition to be proved involves a while loop with initialization, we will apply proof rule W2. By proof rule W2, the correctness proposition above will be true if the following three propositions are true:

$\{n\epsilon Z \text{ and } 0 \le n\}$ k:=1 $\{I\}$ [Proposition 1]

$\{I \text{ and } k \le n \text{ and } A(k) \neq x\}$ k:=k+1 $\{I\}$ [Proposition 2]

$\{I \text{ and } \textbf{not } (k \le n \text{ and } A(k) \neq x)\}$ [Proposition 3]
$\Longrightarrow$
$\{n\epsilon Z \text{ and } k\epsilon Z \text{ and } 1 \le k \le n+1 \text{ and }_{i=1}{}^{k-1} A(i) \neq x$

and $(k \le n$ **and** $A(k)=x$ **or** $k=n+1)\}$

Proposition 1: This proof task consists of verifying the correctness of an individual assignment statement as described in section 4.1.1. By proof rule A2, this correctness proposition will be true if

$\{n\epsilon Z \text{ and } 0 \le n\} \Longrightarrow \{I^k{}_1\}$

Written out in full, this expression becomes

$\{n\epsilon Z \text{ and } 0 \le n\}$

$\Longrightarrow \{n\epsilon Z \text{ and } 1\epsilon Z \text{ and } 1 \le 1 \le n+1 \text{ and }_{i=1}{}^0 A(i) \neq x\}$

The **and** series is empty and has, therefore, the value true (see Appendix A, section A.5). The right part of the implication above reduces to the given precondition (the left part of the implication above), so proposition 1 is true.

Proposition 2: Written out in full, proposition 2 is

$$\{n \varepsilon Z \text{ and } k \varepsilon Z \text{ and } 1 \le k \le n+1 \text{ and}_{i=1}^{k-1} A(i) \neq x$$
$$\text{and } k \le n \text{ and } A(k) \neq x\}$$
$$k := k+1$$
$$\{n \varepsilon Z \text{ and } k \varepsilon Z \text{ and } 1 \le k \le n+1 \text{ and}_{i=1}^{k-1} A(i) \neq x\}$$

The precondition in this proposition can be simplified to

$$\{n \varepsilon Z \text{ and } k \varepsilon Z \text{ and } 1 \le k \le n \text{ and}_{i=1}^{k-1} A(i) \neq x \text{ and } A(k) \neq x\}$$
$$=$$
$$\{n \varepsilon Z \text{ and } k \varepsilon Z \text{ and } 1 \le k \le n \text{ and}_{i=1}^{k} A(i) \neq x\}$$

so that proposition 2 can be rewritten as

$$\{n \varepsilon Z \text{ and } k \varepsilon Z \text{ and } 1 \le k \le n \text{ and}_{i=1}^{k} A(i) \neq x\}$$
$$k := k+1$$
$$\{n \varepsilon Z \text{ and } k \varepsilon Z \text{ and } 1 \le k \le n+1 \text{ and}_{i=1}^{k-1} A(i) \neq x\}$$

By proof rule A2, this correctness proposition will be true if

$$\{n \varepsilon Z \text{ and } k \varepsilon Z \text{ and } 1 \le k \le n \text{ and}_{i=1}^{k} A(i) \neq x\}$$
$$\Longrightarrow$$
$$\{n \varepsilon Z \text{ and } k \varepsilon Z \text{ and } 1 \le k \le n+1 \text{ and}_{i=1}^{k-1} A(i) \neq x\}_{k+1}^{k}$$

or, equivalently,

$$\{n \varepsilon Z \text{ and } k \varepsilon Z \text{ and } 1 \le k \le n \text{ and}_{i=1}^{k} A(i) \neq x\}$$
$$\Longrightarrow$$
$$\{n \varepsilon Z \text{ and } k \varepsilon Z \text{ and } 0 \le k \le n \text{ and}_{i=1}^{k} A(i) \neq x\}$$

which is clearly true. Therefore, proposition 2 is true. More formally,

$\{n\epsilon Z$ and $k\epsilon Z$ and $1\leq k\leq n$ and $_{i=1}^{k}$ A(i)$\neq$x$\}$

$=$
    $(1\leq k)$ and $\{n\epsilon Z$ and $k\epsilon Z$ and $0\leq k\leq n$ and $_{i=1}^{k}$ A(i)$\neq$x$\}$

$\Longrightarrow$
    $\{n\epsilon Z$ and $k\epsilon Z$ and $0\leq k\leq n$ and $_{i=1}^{k}$ A(i)$\neq$x$\}$

Proposition 3: Written out fully, this proposition is:

$\{n\epsilon Z$ and $k\epsilon Z$ and $1\leq k\leq n+1$ and $_{i=1}^{k-1}$ A(i)$\neq$x

and not $(k\leq n$ and $A(k)\neq x)\}$

$\Longrightarrow$

$\{n\epsilon Z$ and $k\epsilon Z$ and $1\leq k\leq n+1$ and $_{i=1}^{k-1}$ A(i)$\neq$x

and $(k\leq n$ and $A(k)=x$ or $k=n+1)\}$

The left part of the implication above can be rewritten as follows (see Appendix A, section A.3, identities 19 and 17, and section A.4, exercise 3):

$\{n\epsilon Z$ and $k\epsilon Z$ and $1\leq k\leq n+1$ and $_{i=1}^{k-1}$ A(i)$\neq$x

and $(k>n$ or $k\leq n$ and $A(k)=x)\}$

$=$
$\{n\epsilon Z$ and $k\epsilon Z$ and $1\leq k\leq n+1$ and $_{i=1}^{k-1}$ A(i)$\neq$x

and $(k\leq n$ and $A(k)=x$ or $k=n+1)\}$

This last expression is the right part of the implication of proposition 3. Proposition 3 is thereby verified.

Total correctness: We have proved above that the given subprogram is partially correct. To prove that it is totally correct, we must still show that it will be executed to completion without a run time error (i.e., that it will "terminate") or, alternatively, identify additional conditions which ensure that it terminates.

Among other things, we must show that the body of the loop will be executed only a limited number of times (finitely many times). In this case – and typically – this part of the proof is relatively simple. Each execution of the loop body increases the value of k by 1. As soon as k>n the loop ends.

In addition, we must show that every execution of every statement in the program will yield a defined result, i.e. that no run time error can arise. In complete detail, such a proof depends upon the target system upon which the program is to run. Despite this fact, however, typically valid conclusions can be drawn (see chapter 2). Strictly speaking, we must also show that every statement is syntactically correct, but we will not concern ourselves here with tests so specific to the target programming language – tests which most systems conduct automatically and completely anyway.

The results of executing the two assignment statements k:=... will always be defined if the (possibly automatically) declared range of the variable k includes all integers from 1 to n+1 inclusive (cf. the loop invariant). If, for example, k and n are declared as variables of the same type, n is not permitted to have the highest value.

The first part of the while condition can always be evaluated if the variables k and n are declared and their values can be compared for ≤. Because k and n take on integer values only (see the loop invariant), the latter condition will be fulfilled. (These variables need not, however, be declared as type integer.)

The second part of the while condition can be evaluated if the variables A(1), ... A(n) and x are declared (or will be automatically declared when needed) and their values can be compared with one another for equality. Furthermore, we must consider that A(n+1) is referenced during the last execution of the loop, for the loop invariant permits k=n+1. When the (possibly undeclared) variable A(n+1) is compared, the term k≤n is false, so that the value of A(n+1) is of no consequence. We must pay attention, however, to the way in which the target system evaluates an expression of the form "false **and** undefined" (see the comments on evaluating an expression in section 2.1). If the target system evaluates this expression as false, then this subprogram will execute without a run time error. If, on the other hand, the target system considers the value of this expression to be undefined, then the execution of this subprogram will end abnormally with a corresponding error message;

with respect to such a system, our subprogram is not totally correct.

A precondition for which the given subprogram is totally correct is, therefore:

- The variable n is declared and has a nonnegative integer value and

- the variable k is declared or will be declared automatically as needed and

- the (possibly automatically) declared range of the variable k includes all integers between 1 and n+1 inclusive and

- the variables A(1), ... A(n) (and, depending upon the target system, A(n+1), see above) and x are declared and their values can be compared with one another for equality.

Additional conditions could be imposed by specific characteristics of the target system upon which the subprogram is to be executed (e.g., that k must be declared as an array subscript variable or as type integer, etc.). ∎

4.4.2 Correctness proof (loop invariant unknown)

In section 4.4.1 it was assumed that a suitable loop invariant was given together with the correctness proposition to be proved. Sometimes, however, one is faced with the task of proving a loop correct even though the loop invariant is unknown. In this case a suitable loop invariant must be determined before the proof can be completed.

The loop invariant is a generalization of the pre- and postconditions of the while loop (see section 3.3.9). I.e., it must be true both before and after execution of the loop.

A loop invariant appropriate for a given loop with initialization and a given postcondition can often be determined as follows. Consider the value of the postcondition initially (i.e. immediately before execution of the loop) and ask how the postcondition would have to be changed in order to be true initially. Terms which prevent the postcondition from being true initially are candidates for omission or modification.

Consider again the example in section **4.4.1**, but without the loop invariant given there.

Example: The given postcondition is:

> $n \epsilon Z$ and $k \epsilon Z$ and $1 \le k \le n+1$ [range of k]
>
> and $\underset{i=1}{\overset{k-1}{\text{and}}} A(i) \neq x$ [all elements before the k-th $\neq$ x]
>
> and $(k \le n$ and $A(k) = x$ [A(k) = x]
>
> or $k = n+1)$ [no element of A = x]

The initialization of the loop ensures that k=1 immediately before execution of the loop begins. The value of the postcondition before the loop is, therefore,

> $n \epsilon Z$ and $1 \epsilon Z$ and $1 \le 1 \le n+1$
>
> and $\underset{i=1}{\overset{0}{\text{and}}} A(i) \neq x$
>
> and $(1 \le n$ and $A(1) = x$
>
> or $1 = n+1)$

which can be simplified to

> $n \epsilon Z$ and $0 \le n$
>
> and $(1 \le n$ and $A(1) = x$
>
> or $0 = n)$

The given precondition of the subprogram ensures that the first line above will be true. However, initially it will not be known if A(1)=x or not. Furthermore, the value of n can be zero or positive. Thus, the last two lines of the postcondition prevent it from being true initially. We can generalize (weaken) the postcondition by omitting these last two lines (which constitute an **and**ed term in the postcondition). The loop invariant I then becomes

> $n \epsilon Z$ and $k \epsilon Z$ and $1 \le k \le n+1$ [range of k]
>
> and $\underset{i=1}{\overset{k-1}{\text{and}}} A(i) \neq x$ [all elements before the k-th $\neq$ x]

(See the example in section **4.4.1**.) ■

The topic of determining the loop invariant is dealt with in more detail in chapter 5.

4.5 APPLYING THE DIVIDE AND CONQUER PROOF RULES

Sometimes a lengthy expression arises in a correctness proof. Although this does not pose a fundamental problem, it can lead to a disorganized, unclear proof. Furthermore, manipulating lengthy algebraic expressions can become quite tedious and difficult. By applying the proof rules DC1 through DC4 ("divide and conquer"), these potential problems can often be avoided.

Example: Consider the following loop, which merges the values from the two presorted arrays A and B into array C,

```
while ia≤na or ib≤nb do
   if ib>nb or ia≤na and A(ia)≤B(ib)
   then C(ic):=A(ia)
           ia:=ia+1
   else  C(ic):=B(ib)
           ib:=ib+1
   endif
   ic:=ic+1
endwhile
```

for which the programmer specified as the loop invariant I

I1:	$1 \leq ia \leq na+1$	[range of ia]
I2:	and $1 \leq ib \leq nb+1$	[range of ib]
I3:	and $(ic-1)=(ia-1)+(ib-1)$	[relationship between ia, ib and ic]

I4:   **and** (ic≤1 **or** ia>na **or** C(ic-1)≤A(ia))
        [next element of A (if any) ≥ last element of C (if any)]

I5:   **and** (ic≤1 **or** ib>nb **or** C(ic-1)≤B(ib))
        [next element of B (if any) ≥ last element of C (if any)]

I6:   **and** $\prod_{i=1}^{ic-2}$ C(i)≤C(i+1)   [C sorted]

I7:   **and** $\prod_{i=1}^{na-1}$ A(i)≤A(i+1) **and** $\prod_{i=1}^{nb-1}$ B(i)≤B(i+1)
                                                                          [A, B sorted]

whose several terms he named as shown above. The lengthiest part of the proof consists of verifying the invariance of the loop invariant I, i.e., that

> {I **and** (ia≤na **or** ib≤nb)}
> **if** ib>nb **or** ia≤na **and** A(ia)≤B(ib)
> **then** C(ic):=A(ia)
>   ia:=ia+1
> **else** C(ic):=B(ib)
>   ib:=ib+1
> **endif**
> ic:=ic+1
> {I}

This program segment consists of a sequence of two statements (an if statement and an assignment statement). Therefore, we apply proof rule S1 and decompose the correctness proposition above into two new propositions:

> {I **and** (ia≤na **or** ib≤nb)}
> **if** ib>nb **or** ia≤na **and** A(ia)≤B(ib)
> **then** C(ic):=A(ia)
>   ia:=ia+1
> **else** C(ic):=B(ib)
>   ib:=ib+1
> **endif**
> {I^{ic}_{ic+1}}

and

> {I^{ic}_{ic+1}} ic:=ic+1 {I}

whereby we obtain I^{ic}_{ic+1} by replacing the variable ic by the expression (ic+1) in I (see proof rule A1).

The last proposition above is true by proof rule A1. We must still decompose the above correctness proposition about the if statement by applying proof rule IF1. After simplifying the preconditions we obtain the following propositions to be proved:

$\{$I **and** ia≤na **and** (ib>nb **or** A(ia)≤B(ib))$\}$
C(ic):=A(ia)
ia:=ia+1
$\{I^{ic}_{ic+1}\}$

and

$\{$I **and** ib≤nb **and** (ia>na **or** B(ib)<A(ia))$\}$
C(ic):=B(ib)
ib:=ib+1
$\{I^{ic}_{ic+1}\}$

The postcondition is a long expression with the same form and structure as the loop invariant I (see above). The algebraic manipulation and the proof are clearer and easier to follow and understand if we decompose the above propositions by applying proof rule DC3. We thereby obtain the propositions

$\{$I **and** ia≤na **and** (ib>nb **or** A(ia)≤B(ib))$\}$
C(ic):=A(ia)
ia:=ia+1
$\{I1^{ic}_{ic+1}\} = \{1 \le ia \le na+1\}$

and

$\{$I **and** ia≤na **and** (ib>nb **or** A(ia)≤B(ib))$\}$
C(ic):=A(ia)
ia:=ia+1
$\{I2^{ic}_{ic+1}\} = \{1 \le ib \le nb+1\}$

and

$\{$I **and** ia≤na **and** (ib>nb **or** A(ia)≤B(ib))$\}$
C(ic):=A(ia)
ia:=ia+1
$\{I3^{ic}_{ic+1}\} = \{(ic)=(ia-1)+(ib-1)\}$

etc. We have 14 propositions of this form to prove, but each is relatively short and simple. Several of them are, in fact, trivial. Each can be proved by applying proof rules S1, A1 and A2 (see section 4.3). Because of the symmetry between ia and ib, etc., structurally identical algebraic transformations arise pairwise, effectively halving the actual work to be done.

Exercise:

1. The given while loop and its loop invariant are almost symmetrical with respect to the arrays A and B and their associated variables ia, ib, na and nb. The two correctness propositions about the then and else branches of the if statement are symmetrical except for the relation between A(ia) and B(ib) (< instead of ≤ in one place). How can complete symmetry be achieved?
2. Formulate in complete detail all 14 correctness propositions obtained by applying proof rule DC3 to the two correctness propositions mentioned above.
3. Prove all of these 14 correctness propositions. ■

4.6 THE SUBPROGRAM OR PROGRAM SEGMENT

The postcondition of a program segment or of a call to a subprogram typically includes two subconditions. One subcondition relates to the effect of executing the program segment or subprogram in question. The other subcondition references variables whose values are not changed by the program segment under consideration. The latter subcondition relates to the effects of previous parts of the program whose results must be preserved for subsequent use. (Cf. proof rules SP1, SP2 and SP3 in sections 3.3.15 through 3.3.17.)

The following example, in which three subprograms are called one after the other, illustrates how the two types of subconditions mentioned above are separated and handled in the proof. The reader should pay particularly close attention to that part of the proof which deals with the second call.

Example: The following part of a program has the task of copying the values in the arrays A and B into array C in such a way that afterward, array C is sorted. Initially, the arrays A and B are not necessarily sorted. The variables na, nb and nc indicate the number of elements in the arrays A, B and C re-

spectively. The correctness proposition to be proved here is as
follows:

> {na≥0 **and** nb≥0}   [ranges of na, nb]
> **call** sortA
> **call** sortB
> **call** merge
>
> {nc=na+nb **and**$_{i=1}^{nc-1}$ C(i)≤C(i+1)}   [C sorted]

This program is a sequence of three statements. Therefore,
we apply proof rule S1 and decompose our proof task into three
subtasks:

> {na≥0 **and** nb≥0} **call** sortA {P1} ?   [Subtask 1, P1 still
>   to be derived]
>
> {P1?} **call** sortB {P2}   [Subtask 2, P2 still to be derived]
>
> {P2?} **call** merge   [Subtask 3]
>
> {nc=na+nb **and**$_{i=1}^{nc-1}$ C(i)≤C(i+1)}

Preconditions are to be determined for the last two statements
in the sequence. For the first statement, the given precondition
is to be verified.

As usual in the case of a sequence of statements, we begin
with the last statement in the sequence.

Subtask 3: The given specification of the subprogram *merge*
states that it (1) calculates the value of the variable nc and (2)
copies the values of the variables A(1), ... A(na), B(1), ... B(nb)
into array C so that array C is sorted. The prerequisite for the
correct functioning of this subprogram is that each of the
arrays A and B is sorted. Formally,

> {na≥0 **and** nb≥0 **and**$_{i=1}^{na-1}$ A(i)≤A(i+1)
>
> **and**$_{i=1}^{nb-1}$ B(i)≤B(i+1)}
>
> **call** merge {nc=na+nb **and**$_{i=1}^{nc-1}$ C(i)≤C(i+1)}

The postcondition of subtask 3 and the postcondition in the specification of the subprogram *merge* are identical. We can, therefore, take the precondition from the specification as the desired precondition P2.

Subtask 2: Now that P2 has been determined (see subtask 3 above), subtask 2 becomes:

$\{$P1?$\}$ **call** sortB
$\{$na≥ 0 **and** nb≥ 0 **and**$_{i=1}^{na-1}$ A$(i)\leq$A$(i+1)$

and$_{i=1}^{nb-1}$ B$(i)\leq$B$(i+1)\}$

The given formal specification of subprogram *sortB* states that it exchanges (permutes, rearranges − i.e. changes) the values of the variables B(1), ... B(nb) and changes the values of the program variables i, j and k. (The values of the variables i, j and k are meaningful only within the subprogram.) Subprogram *sortB* does not modify any other variable. It fulfills the correctness proposition (specification)

$\{$nb$\geq 0\}$ **call** sortB $\{$**and**$_{i=1}^{nb-1}$ B$(i)\leq$B$(i+1)\}$

Our task is to find a precondition for a postcondition which is stronger than the postcondition in the specification. We must, therefore, separate the postcondition of subtask 2 into two subconditions such that one subcondition is identical to (or follows from) the postcondition in the specification and the other subcondition references only variables which are not modified by subprogram *sortB*. In other words, we separate the postcondition of subtask 2 into subconditions corresponding to the conditions P and B in proof rule SP2 (or SP3). (See proof rules SP2 and SP3.) Subtask 2 then becomes

$\{$P1?$\}$ **call** sortB
$\{$na≥ 0 **and** nb≥ 0 **and**$_{i=1}^{na-1}$ A$(i)\leq$A$(i+1)$ [B: not changed
                                by sortB]

and$_{i=1}^{nb-1}$ B$(i)\leq$B$(i+1)\}$ [P: changed by sortB]

We wish to find a precondition by applying proof rule SP2. The conditions V, P and B appearing in proof rule SP2 correspond to the subexpressions above as follows:

V: $nb \geq 0$

P: $\textbf{and}_{i=1}^{nb-1} \ B(i) \leq B(i+1)$

B: $na \geq 0$ **and** $nb \geq 0$ **and**$_{i=1}^{na-1} \ A(i) \leq A(i+1)$

The postcondition in subtask 2 is (P **and** B). By proof rule SP2, the precondition is (V **and** B). The correctness proposition for this call – with the precondition P1 in the desired form – is, therefore,

$\{na \geq 0$ **and** $nb \geq 0$ **and**$_{i=1}^{na-1} \ A(i) \leq A(i+1)\}$ [P1: V **and** B]

call sortB

$\{na \geq 0$ **and** $nb \geq 0$ **and**$_{i=1}^{na-1} \ A(i) \leq A(i+1)$ [B: not changed by sortB]

and$_{i=1}^{nb-1} \ B(i) \leq B(i+1)\}$ [P: changed by sortB]

Subtask 1: Now that P1 has been determined (see subtask 2 above), subtask 1 calls for us to verify that

$\{na \geq 0$ **and** $nb \geq 0\}$ **call** sortA

$\{na \geq 0$ **and** $nb \geq 0$ **and**$_{i=1}^{na-1} \ A(i) \leq A(i+1)\}$

The given formal specification of subprogram *sortA* corresponds to that of subprogram *sortB* (see above). Subprogram *sortA* exchanges (permutes, rearranges – i.e. changes) the values of the variables $A(1), \ldots A(na)$ and changes the values of the internal program variables i, j and k. Subprogram *sortA* does not modify any other variable. It fulfills the correctness proposition (specification)

$\{na \geq 0\}$ **call** sortA $\{\textbf{and}_{i=1}^{na-1} \ A(i) \leq A(i+1)\}$

Here, too, the postcondition in our proof task is stronger than the postcondition in the specification. We must, therefore, separate the postcondition of our proof task as we did in subtask 2 above. (See proof rules SP2 and SP3.) Rewriting subtask 1 accordingly, we must verify that {na≥0 **and** nb≥0} **call** sortA

{na≥0 **and** nb≥0   [B: not changed by sortA]

$\text{and}_{i=1}^{na-1} A(i) \le A(i+1)$}   [P: changed by sortA]

According to proof rule SP2, this correctness proposition is true. In this application of proof rule SP2, the conditions V, P and B appearing therein correspond to the subexpressions above as follows:

V: na≥0

P: $\text{and}_{i=1}^{na-1} A(i) \le A(i+1)$

B: na≥0 **and** nb≥0

This completes the proof (verification) of the original correctness proposition about the sequence of three calls to subprograms. ∎

If the postcondition of a call to a subprogram (or of a program segment) cannot be separated as above (i.e. as required in order to apply proof rule SP2 or SP3), then a design error is present. Either the program contains an error or the formal specification of the subprogram (or program segment) in question is incomplete.

4.7 SUMMARY: PROGRAM ANALYSIS AND VERIFICATION

In order to prove a program or program segment partially correct, one first writes the proof task as a correctness proposition of the form

{V} S {P}

where V is the known (given) precondition, P is the given postcondition and S is the program in question. The proof rule appropriate for S (see the table in section 3.4 and the reference card) is then applied in order to decompose the original correctness proposition to be proved into subsidiary correctness propositions (proof tasks). This process is continued iteratively until only propositions about assignment statements remain.

Finally, these last propositions are verified by applying proof rules A1 and A2 for the assignment statement.

This process decomposes correctness propositions (proof tasks) about larger parts of the program into correctness propositions about ever smaller parts of the program, until the level of individual assignment statements is reached. Thus, the correctness proof is decomposed in a manner reflecting the structure of the program being verified.

When, in the course of decomposing proof tasks in this way, already verified correctness propositions are encountered, one can, of course, stop there. This situation will arise especially in the case of propositions about subprogram calls. (See section 4.6.) Such already verified correctness propositions represent lemmas and theorems about subsidiary parts of the program which each correctness proof for a superior (e.g. calling) program segment may – and should – reference.

To prove additionally that a program is totally correct, one must above all show that the body of each loop will be executed a finite number of times only (i.e. that the number of executions is limited). One must show further that every execution of each statement will yield a defined result, i.e. that no run time error can occur. Chapter 2 contains typically valid guidelines for assessing program statements in this regard. (See section 4.4.1 for an example.)

5

DESIGNING A CORRECT PROGRAM

In this chapter we will design several program segments. Each will be designed to fulfill a given specification – consisting of a precondition and a postcondition. The various requirements of a correctness proof serve as guidelines for the design of the program. They enable us, in fact, to derive several parts of our program more or less directly.

The resulting approach presented here directs the designer's attention to the essential aspects of the program being designed and away from inessential aspects. Consequently, he proceeds more directly and systematically toward his goal than before. The result is often a surprisingly compact program with a simple, clear and logical structure.

This approach contrasts sharply with the traditional way of programming. One views the program and the process of developing it in a rather different way and from a quite different standpoint. In contrast to the traditional approach, one pays more attention to *states* and to that which does not change (to *invariants* and *conditions*), and much less attention to the *changes* brought about by the execution of the program statements. This new, different design approach – and different way of thinking – must be learned and practiced before one can apply it with ease, but experience shows that it is not particularly difficult to master.

With practice and experience, the approach to designing programs presented in this chapter can be employed quickly and easily. The designer applies the various proof rules almost subconsciously and as reflex actions, just as engineering colleagues in other fields apply their theoretical foundations to practical design tasks.

Because of space limitations we will examine only four examples of limited size in this chapter. The subject of each example is the design of a subprogram on the lowest hierarchical level. For design examples involving hierarchically higher level program segments, including a control program at the top level of a middle sized program system, see [Baber, 1987, chapter 6].

When designing a provably correct program one typically proceeds as follows. Starting with a general description of the task the program is to perform, one adds detail, making the description more specific, and formulates the pre- and postconditions as logical algebraic expressions. Then the designer decides upon the basic structure of his program. If, as is often the case, a loop is chosen, he next decides upon a loop invariant. Based on the difference between the postcondition and the loop invariant, he derives the while condition. Using the loop invariant as a check list, he designs the body of the loop. Finally he completes a proof of correctness for his program design. Typically, many parts of the proof fall out of the design process as a by-product.

The loop invariant is determined by generalizing the pre- and postconditions. This step of the design process can be based on either the algebraic formulas or corresponding diagrams or both. Sometimes the formulas lead more directly to the goal and sometimes diagrams simplify and clarify the process more effectively. The practical software designer should, in any case, develop his ability to use and think in terms of both representational forms fluently and to "translate" between them in both directions.

Frequently the required initialization of the loop becomes obvious during the process of determining the loop invariant.

When reading and studying the following design examples, note carefully how the design steps described generally above are actually carried out in detail.

5.1 DESIGN EXAMPLE: LINEAR SEARCH

In our first example we will design the program segment which was proved correct in section 4.4.1.

The variable n, the array A(1), A(2), ... A(n) and the variable x are given. The program to be designed is to determine whether the value of x is present in the array A and if so, where it first occurs. The value of the result variable k should indicate which element of A was found to be equal to x.

5.1.1 Specification

The precondition is given as

$n \varepsilon Z$ **and** $0 \le n$

The program to be designed should calculate a value for the variable k so that after execution of the program the postcondition

$k \varepsilon Z$ **and** $1 \le k \le n+1$ [range of k]

and $\sum_{i=1}^{k-1} A(i) \ne x$ [all elements before the k-th $\ne$ x]

and $(k \le n$ **and** $A(k)=x$ [A(k) = x]

    or $k=n+1)$ [no element of A = x]

is satisfied (is true). No other variable should be modified.

5.1.2 Basic structure of the subprogram

It seems appropriate and natural to solve the stated problem by comparing elements of the array A, one after the other, with x (testing for equality). The *repetition* of the same basic step suggests a loop for the basic structure of our program. As a rule, a loop has an initialization, which ensures that the loop invariant is true initially. Thus, our program has the general form

> initialization; **while** B **do** S **endwhile**

5.1.3 Loop invariant

The most important design decision in connection with a loop is the determination of the loop invariant. An appropriate loop invariant can be determined by generalizing the postcondition and the initial situation (see section 3.3.9).

In section 4.4.2 we determined a loop invariant for this loop. There, the program − in particular the initialization of the loop − was known. Here we proceed similarly, but we cannot refer to an existing initialization routine for the loop.

We begin with the postcondition (see above) and ask ourselves how it must be generalized (weakened) in order to be satisfied initially. Is or can the first line of the postcondition be true in the beginning? The precondition ensures that $n \geq 0$. If the first line of the postcondition is to be true for all possible values of n, then it must be true that $1 \leq k \leq 0+1$ (assuming that the initial value of k does not depend on n), i.e. $k=1$. Viewed the other way around, the first line of the postcondition will be true if $k=1$. This observation suggests the assignment statement $k:=1$ for the initialization.

If $k=1$, then the second line of the postcondition is the empty **and** series, which by definition is true.

The third line of the postcondition asserts that $A(k)=x$. Initially $(k=1)$ it will be unknown whether $A(k)=x$ or not. Also the fourth line can be either true or false initially. Since these two lines together form an **and**ed term of the postcondition, the postcondition can be weakened by omitting them.

Thus we are left with the following condition as our loop invariant I:

> $k \varepsilon Z$ **and** $1 \leq k \leq n+1$ [range of k]
>
> $\text{and}_{i=1}^{k-1} A(i) \neq x$ [all elements before the k-th $\neq$ x]

The loop invariant I can be represented by the following diagram:

The loop invariant {I}

1	k	n
$\neq$ x		?

Another line of reasoning also leads to this loop invariant. We pose the question, which parts of the postcondition must be true at intermediate stages of the search and which not? The first line of the postcondition limits the range of values of the variable k; the given range includes all values obviously required during the search. Those elements of A already investigated will be unequal to x, so the second line of the postcondition will be true at intermediate stages of the search. During the search neither of the conditions A(k)=x (equality found) or k=n+1 (end of array) will, in general, be true; the last two lines of the postcondition cannot, therefore, be included in a suitable loop invariant.

5.1.4 While condition

In the correctness proof we must show that the postcondition is satisfied upon termination of the loop, in particular, that [I **and not** B] $\Longrightarrow$ the postcondition P (see proof rule W2). We formed the loop invariant by omitting an **and**ed term of the postcondition. The omitted term is an obvious candidate for [**not** B]. Therefore, we negate the omitted term to derive the while condition B:

> **not** [k≤n **and** A(k)=x **or** k=n+1]

=

> [k>n **or** A(k)$\neq$x] **and** k$\neq$n+1

=

[k>n **or** k≤n **and** A(k)≠x] **and** k≠n+1

=

[k>n **and** k≠n+1 **or** k≤n **and** k≠n+1 **and** A(k)≠x]

=

[k>n+1 **or** k≤n **and** A(k)≠x]

The loop invariant will always be true when the while condition is evaluated. It follows that the left term above will always be false. We choose, therefore, for the while condition simply

k≤n **and** A(k)≠x

5.1.5 Loop body

The body of the loop has only two functions to perform: (1) to maintain the truth of the loop invariant and (2) to achieve progress in the direction of termination (the postcondition). Cf. (1) proof rule W1 and step 3 of proof rule W2 – {I **and** B} S {I} – and (2) step 5 of proof rule W2. Any other consideration when designing the loop body is superfluous, because it contributes nothing to the correctness proof.

The following diagram represents the relationships between the values of the variables A(.) and x which are known to be true just before each execution of the loop body {I **and** B}:

The precondition of the loop body {I **and** B}

1		k	k+1		n
	≠		≠	?	

Comparing this diagram for {I **and** B} with the diagram for {I} (see the previous diagram above) we see that the diagram for {I **and** B} can be transformed into the diagram for the loop invariant by increasing k by 1. Examining the corresponding logical algebraic expressions leads to the same conclusion.

Increasing k reduces the length of the unknown region; i.e., progress is made toward termination (fulfilling the postcondition). This observation suggests the length of the unknown region in the loop invariant, i.e. n-k+1, as the loop variant in the formal proof of termination. (See the diagram for {I} above.)

The body of the loop will, therefore, consist of the one assignment statement k:=k+1.

5.1.6 The complete subprogram

Thus the complete subprogram is as follows:

    k:=1
    while k≤n **and** A(k)≠x **do** k:=k+1 **endwhile**

5.1.7 Correctness proof

The correctness of the program designed here was proved in section 4.4.1.

5.2 DESIGN EXAMPLE: PARTITIONING AN ARRAY

The integer variables il and ir and the array variables X(il), X(il+1), ... X(ir) are given. The precondition is not specified in greater detail. Any additional necessary restrictions to be added to the precondition are to be specified by the designer of this subprogram.

The subprogram to be designed should exchange (permute) the values of the above array variables and determine values for the variables gl and gr such that three regions of the array are formed:

The postcondition

il		gl	gr	ir
	<		=	>

The middle region may not be empty; the others are permitted to be empty. The subprogram being designed should select the value of the elements in the middle region. No restrictions are placed on the method for selecting that value.

5.2.1 Specification

Expressed as a logical algebraic expression, the postcondition is as follows:

$il \le gl \le gr \le ir$

$$\textbf{and}_{i=il}^{gl-1} \ X(i) < X(gl)$$

$$\textbf{and}_{i=gl}^{gr} \ X(i) = X(gl)$$

$$\textbf{and}_{i=gr+1}^{ir} \ X(i) > X(gl)$$

The precondition is to be specified in detail by the designer of the subprogram.

5.2.2 Basic structure of the subprogram

It must be assumed that, in general, many exchanges of values of the elements of the array X will be necessary to fulfill the postcondition. The repetition of an operation (here exchanging) suggests that a loop would be an appropriate basic structure for our program.

5.2.3 Loop invariant

The loop invariant I must be true initially as well as finally. The diagram above illustrates the postcondition, i.e. the final situation.

Initially, nothing is known about the relationships between the values of the array elements. A diagram corresponding to that for the postcondition but representing the initial situation is:

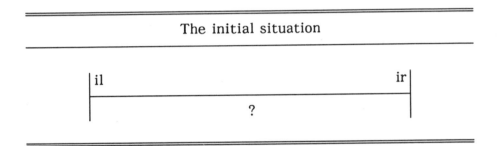

The loop invariant must be a generalization of the initial and final situations (pre- and postconditions). It must, therefore, include the four regions <, =, > and ?. One of the several possibilities is:

The loop invariant {I}

In logical algebraic form, the loop invariant I is

$il \le gl \le gr \le k \le ir$

$$\text{and}_{i=il}^{\quad gl-1} X(i) < X(gl)$$

$$\text{and}_{i=gl}^{\quad gr} X(i) = X(gl)$$

$$\text{and}_{i=k+1}^{\quad ir} X(i) > X(gl)$$

5.2.4 While condition

If $gr \ge k$, then the ? region is empty and the loop invariant implies the postcondition. See the diagrams above for the postcondition and for the loop invariant.

Thus, the end condition for the while loop is $gr \ge k$. The while condition is the negation thereof, i.e. $gr < k$.

5.2.5 Loop body

We must design the body of the loop such that it (1) maintains the truth of the loop invariant and (2) makes progress toward fulfilling the postcondition.

In order to make progress toward fulfilling the postcondition, the size of the ? region in the loop invariant must be reduced (see the diagram above). An element of the ? region – e.g. $X(gr+1)$ – must be selected and inserted into one of the three regions <, = or > as appropriate. By comparing the selected element with any element in the = region, we can determine in which region the selected element belongs. The result of comparing $X(gr+1)$ and $X(gl)$ will be either case 1:

[Case 1]

or case 2:

il		gl	gr		k		ir
	<		=	=	?		>

[Case 2]

or case 3:

il		gl	gr		k		ir
	<		=	>	?		>

[Case 3]

The loop invariant does not correspond to the relevant diagram; the validity of the loop invariant must be re-established. That is the *only* purpose of the other statements which we must write into the loop body. The statements which must be executed in order to re-establish the validity of the loop invariant differ in the three cases above. This case distinction leads to a corresponding structure of if statements in our program.

Case 1:

il		gl	gr		k		ir
	<		=	<	?		>

[Case 1]

Exchanging the values of X(gl) and X(gr+1) brings them to the appropriate places:

il		gl	gr		k		ir
	<	<	=	=	?		>

Increasing gl and gr by 1 establishes a state corresponding to (described by) the loop invariant, i.e. re-establishes the validity of the loop invariant:

il		gl	gr	k		ir
	<		=	?		>

[I after case 1]

Thus in this case the following statements must be executed to re-establish the validity of the loop invariant.

    X(gl):=:X(gr+1)
    gl:=gl+1
    gr:=gr+1

The exchange statement (x:=:y) causes the values of the variables x and y to be exchanged. The previous value of x is assigned to the variable y and the previous value of y is assigned to the variable x. I.e. the previous value of x becomes the subsequent value of y and the previous value of y becomes the subsequent value of x. The same effect can be achieved with the following assignment statements, whereby auxvar is an auxiliary variable not used for any other purpose.

    auxvar:=x
    x:=y
    y:=auxvar

Case 2:

il		gl	gr		k		ir	
	<		=	=	?		>	

[Case 2]

All values are already in the correct places; only the boundary gr must be adjusted by increasing it by 1.

il		gl		gr		k		ir	
	<		=			?		>	

[I after case 2]

In this case only the assignment statement

    gr:=gr+1

must be executed.

Case 3:

il		gl	gr			k		ir	
	<		=		>	?		>	

[Case 3]

Exchanging the values of X(k) and X(gr+1) brings them to the appropriate places:

il		gl	gr			k		ir
	<		=	?	?		>	>

Decreasing k by 1 restores the validity of the loop invariant:

il		gl	gr	k		ir	
	<		=		?		>

[I after case 3]

Thus in this case the assignment statements

    X(k):=:X(gr+1)
    k:=k-1

must be executed.

5.2.6 Initialization

We must design the initialization so that after its execution the loop invariant is true. The loop invariant I states that the = region may not be empty (gl≤gr). The description of the design task stated that the = element may be selected in any convenient way. The < and > regions are initially empty. The ? region contains all elements other than the one chosen as the first = element. Therefore, we write for the initialization

    gl:=il   [< region empty]
    gr:=gl   [= region contains 1 element]
    k:=ir   [> region empty]

The arbitrary selection of the = element can be explicitly expressed by prefixing the exchange statement

    X(il):=:X(j), where j is any integer in the interval il≤j≤ir

to the initialization already designed above.

The initialization establishes the following starting situation:

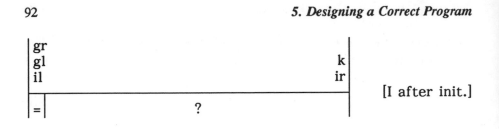

[I after init.]

5.2.7 The complete subprogram

Putting together the various individual parts of the program, all of which we have now designed, the complete program becomes

```
gl:=il; gr:=gl; k:=ir
while gr<k do
    if X(gr+1)<X(gl)
    then X(gl):=:X(gr+1)
            gl:=gl+1
            gr:=gr+1
    else if X(gr+1)=X(gl)
    then gr:=gr+1
    else [Remark: X(gr+1)>X(gl)]
            X(k):=:X(gr+1)
            k:=k-1
    endif
    endif
endwhile
```

5.2.8 Precondition

The precondition of the loop invariant I (as postcondition) with respect to the initialization – which (by proof rule W2) is also the precondition of the entire subprogram – is derived by applying proof rules S1 and A1 to the initialization:

{il≤ir}
gl:=il
gr:=gl
k:=ir
{il≤gl≤gr≤k≤ir

$$\text{and}_{i=il}^{gl-1} \; X(i) < X(gl)$$

$$\text{and}_{i=gl}^{gr} \; X(i) = X(gl)$$

$$\text{and}_{i=k+1}^{ir} \; X(i) > X(gl)\}$$

This precondition makes explicit the requirement that the given array X must contain at least one element − in order that after the execution of the subprogram the middle region can contain at least one element.

5.2.9 Termination of the loop

Does the loop end? The value of the expression (loop variant)

k-gr

which is the length of the ? region in the loop invariant I, is reduced by 1 with each execution of the loop body. The lower bound of this value is 0 (see the loop invariant I and the while condition). The loop must, therefore, terminate after finitely many (i.e. after a limited number of) executions of the loop body.

5.2.10 Correctness proof

The correctness proof for this subprogram reflects closely the several design steps above.

Exercise:

1. How can proof rules A1 and A2 be generalized for the exchange statement (:=:)? How can the exchange statement be handled in a correctness proof?

2. Prove the correctness of the program designed above in section 5.2. ■

See [Baber, 1987, section 6.3] and [Dijkstra, 1976, chapter 14] for variations of this design task.

5.3 DESIGN EXAMPLE: SEARCHING FOR A SUBSTRING

The variables M and N as well as the arrays D and K are given. The values of the variables M and N are integers. The values of the array variables D(.) and K(.) can be compared with one another for equality, but are not specified more precisely (e.g. they may be characters). The program to be designed should search the array D(id), id = 0, 1, ... M-1, for a subsequence equal to the sequence [K(0), K(1), ... K(N-1)]. Typically, the value of N is much less than the value of M.

After the execution of our program the variable j should indicate where the first subsequence of D begins which is equal to the sequence K. If no such subsequence of D is present, the value of j should indicate this situation. A more detailed specification of the program to be designed – e.g. the pre- and postconditions in the form of logical algebraic expressions – is not given.

5.3.1 Preliminary analysis

Which values can the result variable j take on? In other words, at which positions of D can a subsequence begin which is equal to (the entire sequence) K? The sequence D begins in position 0 (D(0)), so the first subsequence of D which could be equal to K begins in position 0. The last subsequence of D which could be equal to K ends in the last position of D, M-1. This subsequence must be of the same length as K; it must, therefore, begin in position M-1-(N-1) = M-N. Every subsequence of D which begins in a later position is too short to be equal to K.

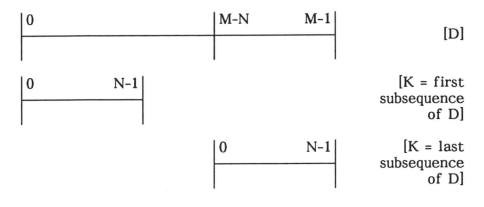

If D is shorter than K (M<N), then no subsequence of D can be equal to K.

If a subsequence of D is found which is equal to K, then the value of j (the starting position in D of the subsequence) must lie in the interval $0 \le j \le M-N$. The program to be designed should find the first subsequence of D which is equal to K. The search must, therefore, begin at position 0 of array D. For this reason, it seems appropriate to define "too large" a value of j (j>M-N) to mean that no subsequence of D is equal to K.

Implicit in these preliminary deliberations is the idea of finding the sequence by repeatedly comparing. The repetition, in turn, suggests a loop as the basic structure for our program.

We will presumably need to talk often about equality and inequality of subsequences of D and K, e.g. in the postcondition, loop invariant, etc. We should, therefore, develop a logical algebraic formula for such equality. The subsequence of D which starts in position s is equal to K when D(s)=K(0) and D(s+1)=K(1) and ... D(s+N-1)=K(N-1), i.e. when

$$\textbf{and}_{a=0}^{N-1} D(s+a)=K(a) \qquad \text{[K = subsequence of D starting at position s]}$$

We will call this condition G(s) below.

The subsequence of D beginning in position s is not equal to K if

$$\text{not } G(s) \qquad\qquad [K \neq \text{subsequence of D beginning at s}]$$

$$=$$

$$\text{not and}_{a=0}^{N-1} \ D(s+a)=K(a)$$

$$=$$

$$\text{or}_{a=0}^{N-1} \ D(s+a){\neq}K(a)$$

5.3.2 Specification

The following assertions must be expressed in the postcondition. Either K has been found in D ($0{\le}j{\le}$M-N) or K is not present in D ($j{>}$M-N), see above. (We exclude the possibility that K is present in D but was not found.) If K was found in D, then the subsequence of D beginning in position j is equal to K. Furthermore, this is the first such subsequence in D; in other words, all previous subsequences of D are not equal to K. The value of j is in any case an integer and at least 0. Thus, our preliminary postcondition is

$$j{\varepsilon}Z \text{ and } 0{\le}j \qquad\qquad \text{[range of j]}$$

$$\text{and}_{k=0}^{j-1} \text{ not } G(k) \qquad\qquad \text{[all subsequences of D}$$
$$\text{before the j-th} \neq K]$$

$$\text{and } (j{>}M{-}N \qquad\qquad \text{[no subsequence of D = K]}$$

$$\text{or } j{\le}M{-}N \text{ and } G(j)) \qquad\qquad \text{[subsequence of D}$$
$$\text{starting at j = K]}$$

No upper boundary for the value of j is given in this postcondition. It is often easier to prove termination if both upper and lower bounds for all variables modified in the loop are known. Therefore the postcondition should, in general, contain both an upper and a lower bound for the value of each variable calculated by the program segment in question.

At first it would appear to suffice to specify M-N+1, the first value greater than M-N, as the maximum value of j. Then the range of j would be $0{\le}j{\le}$M-N+1. But if D is short and K, long, then M-N+1 is negative and this condition cannot be satisfied. We must, therefore, always permit j to be 0. The upper bound on j must, then, be the larger of M-N+1 or 0. Written out completely, our postcondition becomes

$j\varepsilon Z$ and $0 \le j \le \max(0, M-N+1)$ [range of j]

and$_{k=0}^{j-1}$ (or$_{a=0}^{N-1}$ $D(k+a) \ne K(a)$) [subsequences of D before the j-th $\ne$ K]

and (j>M-N [no subsequence of D = K]

or $j \le M-N$ and$_{a=0}^{N-1}$ $D(j+a)=K(a)$) [subsequence of D starting at j = K]

and in diagrammatical form

The postcondition

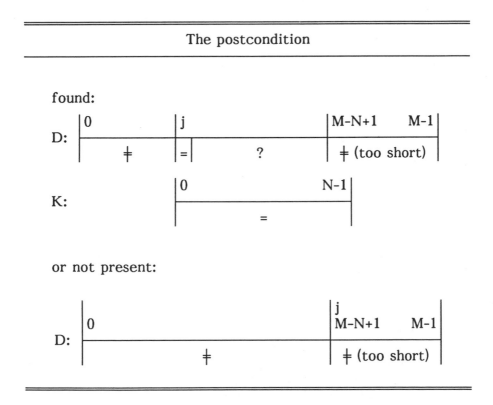

found:

or not present:

In the original description of the design task the precondition was not precisely defined. The variables M and N indicate the lengths of the arrays D and K respectively; only values ≥ 0 are meaningful. It was stated that the value of N is typically much less than the value of M. That does not mean, however, that

N<M must necessarily be true. In fact, it is desirable that our program also functions correctly when a long sequence is being sought in a shorter one (in which case, of course, the result should be "not present"). Thus the preliminary precondition, which we must perhaps revise after designing the program, is

MεZ and 0≤M and NεZ and 0≤N

In a diagrammatical form corresponding to that of the postcondition above, the precondition is

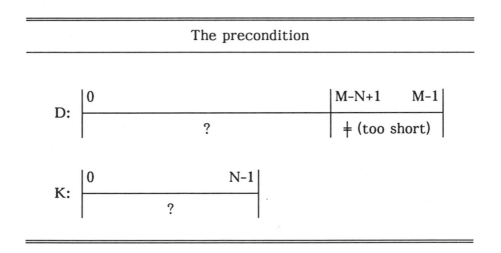

The precondition

5.3.3 Loop invariant

We can determine a suitable loop invariant by generalizing the pre- and postconditions. We can do this on the basis of either the diagrams or the logical algebraic formulas.

Looking at the diagrams for the pre- and postconditions, we notice that a ? region in array K is missing in the postcondition; otherwise the precondition can be viewed as a special case of the postcondition. By extending the postcondition accordingly we obtain for the loop invariant

The loop invariant $\{I\}$

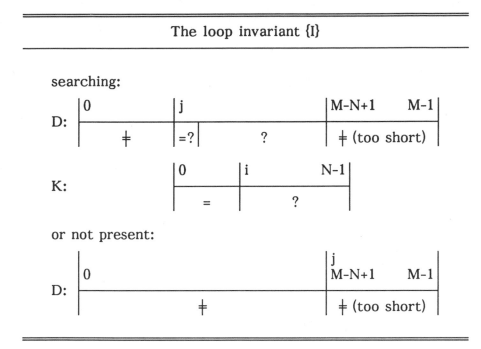

searching:

or not present:

This diagram for the loop invariant can be interpreted as follows. Either the search for sequence K in D is still in progress or it has already been determined that K is not present in D. In the first case (searching), it has already been determined that the subsequences of D which begin in the positions 0, 1, ... j-1 are not equal to K. The subsequence of D which begins in position j is currently being tested for equality to K. Up to position i (exclusively), the subsequences are equal.

Alternatively, we can examine the logical algebraic formulas for the pre- and postconditions and ask ourselves, what part(s) of the postcondition prevent the postcondition from being true initially. Only the value of 0 for j will always satisfy the first line, which suggests that the initialization must ensure that j=0. Then only "N" in the upper limit of the **and** series in the last line prevents the postcondition from being true initially. We must introduce a new variable (e.g. i) in its place which is initialized in such a way that this **and** series is true (i.e. empty). This suggests 0 as the initial value of i.

In addition, an assertion about the range of the newly introduced variable i should be included in the loop invariant. This assertion should be as strong (restrictive) as possible. The initial value 0 (see the last paragraph above) will be the minimum value (lower bound). When i=N, the postcondition is fulfilled. Therefore, we need not allow i to assume greater values.

These considerations lead to our loop invariant I

$j \varepsilon Z$ and $0 \le j \le \max(0, M-N+1)$ and $i \varepsilon Z$ and $0 \le i \le N$

[ranges of i and j]

$$\text{and}_{k=0}^{j-1} \ (\text{or}_{a=0}^{N-1} \ D(k+a) \ne K(a))$$

[subsequences of D before the j-th $\ne$ K]

and $(j > M-N$

[no subsequence of D = K]

$$\text{or} \ j \le M-N \ \text{and}_{a=0}^{i-1} \ D(j+a) = K(a))$$

[subsequence of D starting at j = K to position i-1]

The above comments and observations also lead to the conclusion that the initialization must contain (or consist of) the sequence of assignment statements

i:=0; j:=0

5.3.4 While condition

The loop can be terminated as soon as the postcondition is fulfilled. When does the loop invariant imply the postcondition? Looking at the diagrams above for the postcondition and the loop invariant, we see that the postcondition is fulfilled either when the ? region in K is empty (i>N-1) or when j≥M-N+1. Thus the end condition is

i>N-1 **or** j≥M-N+1

The negation of the end condition is the while condition

i≤N-1 **and** j<M-N+1

or, equivalently, (because i, j, M and N are integers)

i<N **and** j≤M-N

Now that we have designed the initialization and the while condition, only the loop body remains.

5.3.5 Loop body

The body of the loop must (1) make progress toward fulfilling the postcondition (in order that termination can be proved) and (2) maintain the truth of the loop invariant.

Before each execution of the loop body both the loop invariant and the while condition will be true, i.e. {I **and** B} will be true. Thus, in our specific case, the upper part of the diagram for the loop invariant will apply and the ? region in K will not be empty:

The precondition of the loop body {I **and** B}

---

searching:

Progress toward fulfilling the postcondition can be made by increasing i or j. Because the truth of the loop invariant must be maintained, the variable i may be increased only if the corresponding elements of the arrays D and K are equal, i.e. if D(j+i)=K(i). This observation suggests an if statement with this condition. The variable j may be increased only if the subsequence of D beginning in position j is not equal to K – e.g. because D(j+i)≠K(i). In this case, the variable i must be reset to 0 in order to ensure the truth of the loop invariant.

The loop body, therefore, consists of the following if statement:

> **if** $D(j+i)=K(i)$ **then** i:=i+1 **else** j:=j+1; i:=0 **endif**

5.3.6 The complete subprogram

Assembling the various parts of the program designed above, we have for our complete subprogram

> i:=0; j:=0
> **while** i<N **and** j≤M-N **do**
>   **if** $D(j+i)=K(i)$ **then** i:=i+1 **else** j:=j+1; i:=0 **endif**
> **endwhile**

5.3.7 Precondition

In the original description of the design task the precondition was not precisely defined. The preliminary version of the precondition worked out in section 5.3.2 is subject to verification or revision. Therefore, we will now derive a precondition for our program. The loop invariant I must be true after the initialization (see proof rule W2). A precondition of I with respect to the initialization is (see proof rules S1 and A1)

$$(I^j_0)^i_0 = (0≤N)$$

The precondition assumed in section 5.3.2 is stronger and therefore, by proof rule P1, also a precondition with respect to the program designed here.

Exercise:

1. What is the meaning of N=0? M=0? What does our program do and what does the postcondition mean in these cases?
2. The precondition derived in section 5.3.7 permits M<0. Interpret the postcondition and the effect of executing the program in this case.
3. The term j≤max(0,M-N+1) appears in the loop invariant. Show that in general

   $$[j≤max(a,b)] = [j≤a \text{ or } j≤b]$$

and

$$[j \le min(a,b)] = [j \le a \text{ and } j \le b]$$

4. Prove the correctness of the program designed above. ∎

5.4 DESIGN EXAMPLE: LOCATING THE NEXT NAME IN AN ARRAY OF STRINGS

An array is given, each element of which is a string (a sequence of characters). An array variable is also called a "line" in this subchapter. The given array of lines contains names. A name is a sequence of one or more characters other than the space. One or more consecutive spaces separate names. A name is always contained in one line, i.e. a line break separates names.

The program to be designed should locate the first name which begins in or after a given position. The name found (if any) should be returned to the calling program as the result.

The input variables to the program to be designed are A (the array), n (the number of lines in array A), bl (beginning line number) and bp (beginning position number). The array consists of the array variables A(1), A(2), ... A(n). The search is to begin in position bp of A(bl).

An array could, for example, appear as follows, whereby the symbol ∎ marks the end of a line. In this example, n=3.

```
A(1):    input1     input5          output1    ∎
A(2):    input3     input7     output3∎
A(3):input2    input4     output4    ∎
```

A line may be empty, i.e. may be 0 characters long. A line may contain only spaces. The array may be empty (n=0).

5.4.1 Preliminary analysis

We will find it necessary to refer often to a specific position of a specific line. We should, therefore, establish a uniform convention for such references. In particular, we should identify the ranges of values of the (integer) position and line numbers.

In any case we must allow line numbers from 1 to n inclusive. This range is not sufficient, however, e.g. when n=0. In order to cover this case, the range of permissible line numbers must either begin with 0 or extend to n+1. We choose the latter:

   1 ≤ line number ≤ n+1

Correspondingly we establish the convention that position numbers begin with 1 and end with the length of the line in question plus 1:

   1 ≤ position number ≤ length(A(line number))+1

where "length" is a function, assumed to be given, whose value is the number of characters in the argument string. This condition is meaningful only when the line number refers to a line actually present, i.e. when 1≤line number≤n. Otherwise, i.e. when the line number=n+1, it would seem appropriate to define the range of the position number as if the (fictitious) line were empty, in other words, as if it were of length 0. In this case the position number must be 1.

We further assume that a function exists in the target programming language which extracts a substring from a given string. We call this function "mid" and assume that mid(S,p,len) is the substring which begins in position p of the string S and is len characters long. Furthermore, we assume that this function counts the positions in a string beginning with 1 (not 0).

5.4.2 Specification

The input variables for the subprogram to be designed are n, the array A, bl and bp (see the general description of the program above). We assume that the values of bl and bp are valid line and position numbers. Thus the precondition is

n∈Z and bl∈Z and bp∈Z	[n, bl, bp integers]
and 0≤n and 1≤bl≤n+1	[ranges of n, bl]
and (bl=n+1 and bp=1	[at end of array]
or bl≤n and 1≤bp≤length(A(bl))+1)	[inside array]

Because no precise postcondition was given, we must formulate it. The task of the subprogram is to locate the first name which begins in or after the position (bl,bp), whereby we must allow for the possibility that no such name is present. Spaces and line breaks may be present before the first name begins. The name found (if any) should be returned to the calling program as one of the results of the subprogram.

First, we must distinguish between two possibilities: no name is present in or after position (bl,bp) or (at least) one is present.

No name is present when the entire area from the position (bl,bp) to the end of the array − position (n+1,1) − contains only spaces and line breaks. We will write this condition below as "empty(bl,bp,n+1,1)". When no further name is present, the result returned to the calling program should indicate this situation, e.g. by being the empty string.

If a name is present, our subprogram must locate its beginning and end. We will use the variables nl and np to record the line and position respectively in which the name begins. The area between the position (bl,bp) and the beginning of the name (nl,np) must, of course, be empty. We will use the variable ep to record the name's end position (which must be in the same line as the beginning position). The result of the subprogram, then, must be the name lying between these two positions.

The following diagram represents the postcondition.

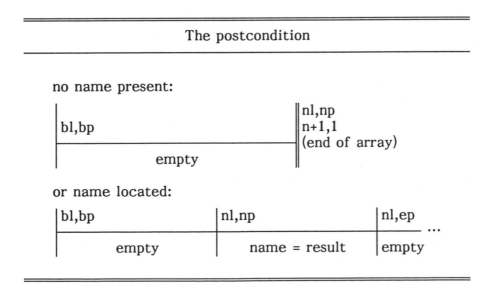

The postcondition

no name present:

bl,bp ———————————— empty ———————————— nl,np / n+1,1 / (end of array)

or name located:

bl,bp ——— empty ——— nl,np ——— name = result ——— nl,ep / empty ...

Expressed in the form of a logical algebraic expression, the postcondition is

     empty(bl,bp,nl,np)   [empty zone before name]

     and {nl=n+1 **and** result=empty string   [no name present]
         or
         nl≤n **and** nameloc(nl,np,ep)   [name located]
         and result=mid(A(nl),np,ep-np)}

Formally we must still define the functions empty(...) and nameloc(...) and include restrictions on the ranges of the variables nl, np and ep in the postcondition above.

Exercise:

1. Supplement the postcondition above with assertions about the ranges of the variables nl, np and ep.
2. Define formally the functions empty(...) and nameloc(...).
3. It might be desirable to require in the precondition that the position (bl,bp) does not lie inside a name. Supplement the precondition with a corresponding assertion. ■

5.4.3 Basic structure of the subprogram

It seems appropriate to establish the truth of the several **and**ed terms in the postcondition (see above) step by step, one after the other. In the first step, our subprogram scans over spaces and line breaks until either the beginning of a name or the end of the array is encountered. The results of this first step are the values of the variables nl and np. In the second step, the end of the name (if any is present) is located. The result of the second step is the value of the variable ep. In the last step, the result of the subprogram – the name found or the empty string – is assigned to the output variable.

The basic structure of the subprogram will, therefore, be a sequence of statements. The first and second steps will each consist primarily of a loop.

5.4.4 Step 1: Locating the end of the empty region

We begin planning this part of our program, as usual, with its goal, i.e. its postcondition. The postcondition of the first step — locating the end of the empty region — is

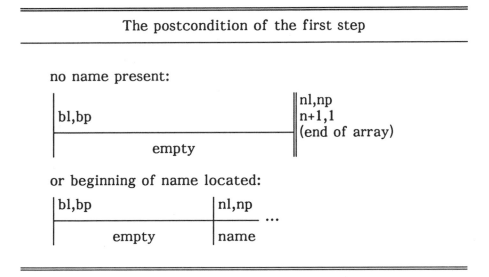

The postcondition of the first step

no name present:

or beginning of name located:

The main part of our loop invariant will be the assertion that the region from position (bl,bp) until just before position (nl,np) is empty, i.e. contains at most spaces and line breaks. Also part of the loop invariant is the requirement that the values of the variables nl and np are in the allowed ranges for line and position numbers (see section 5.4.1 above).

The initial truth of the loop invariant can be established by setting the values of nl and np to bl and bp respectively.

Our loop should end when either (1) the end of the array is encountered (nl=n+1) or (2) the beginning of a name — a character other than a space within a line within the array — is encountered:

nl>n
or nl≤n **and** np≤length(A(nl)) **and** mid(A(nl),np,1)≠space

or equivalently

nl>n **or** np≤length(A(nl)) **and** mid(A(nl),np,1)≠space

The negation of this end condition is the while condition:

nl≤n **and** (np>length(A(nl)) **or** mid(A(nl),np,1)=space)

Only the body of the loop remains to be designed. The while condition will be true if and only if a line break or a space occurs at position (nl,np). The loop body should skip over this position in such a way that the truth of the loop invariant is maintained. In particular, the values of nl and np must remain in the allowed range. If a line break was encountered, then nl must be increased by 1 and np must be set to 1. If a space was found, np should be increased by 1. Thus the first part of our program becomes

```
nl:=bl; np:=bp
while nl≤n and (np>length(A(nl))
                    or mid(A(nl),np,1)=space) do
   if np>length(A(nl))
   then nl:=nl+1; np:=1 else np:=np+1 endif
endwhile
```

5.4.5 Step 2: Locating the end of the name

The postcondition of the second step − locating the end of the name − is

The postcondition of the second step

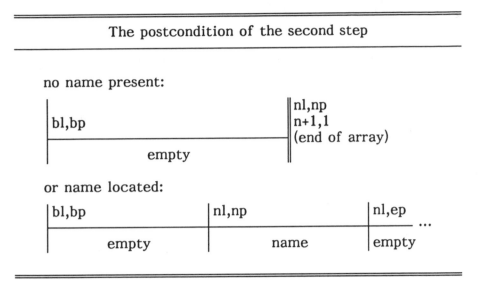

no name present:

or name located:

Our precondition for this second step is the postcondition of the previous (first) step. In particular, valid values have already been calculated for the variables nl and np. If nl=n+1, then the postcondition of the second step is already satisfied, so nothing further need be done (in this step). Otherwise (nl≤n) the end of the name must be located. This case distinction suggests an if statement.

The end of the name can be located by skipping over all characters belonging to the name. This idea suggests repeated comparisons with a space. The repetition in turn suggests a loop. The loop invariant is obvious: every position from (nl,np) to just before (nl,ep) contains a character other than a space. Also part of the loop invariant is the requirement that the value of the variable ep is in the allowed range for a position number for line nl.

The initial truth of the loop invariant can be established by setting the value of ep to either np or np+1.

The loop should end when position (nl,ep) no longer belongs to the name. This will be the case as soon as either the end of the line is reached (ep>length(A(nl))) or position (nl,ep) contains a space:

ep>length(A(nl)) **or** mid(A(nl),ep,1)=space

The while condition is the negation thereof:

ep≤length(A(nl)) **and** mid(A(nl),ep,1)≠space

The loop body should bring position (nl,ep), which contains a character other than a space, into the name region. This is simply done by increasing the value of the variable ep by 1 (see the loop invariant above).

Thus the second part of our program becomes

```
if nl≤n
then ep:=np+1
        while ep≤length(A(nl)) and mid(A(nl),ep,1)≠space do
            ep:=ep+1
        endwhile
endif
```

5.4.6 Step 3: Determining the result

The task of the third and last part of our program is to determine the value of the result variable. If a name was found, then the result should be the substring which begins in position (nl,np) and ends in position (nl,ep-1). Otherwise (if no name is present), the result should be the empty string. This case distinction suggests an if statement. The last part of the program to be designed is, therefore:

```
if nl≤n
then result:=mid(A(nl),np,ep-np)
else result:=empty string
endif
```

5.4.7 The complete subprogram

Bringing the individual steps together and combining the if statements of the second and third parts, the complete program becomes

```
nl:=bl; np:=bp
while nl≤n and (np>length(A(nl))
                or mid(A(nl),np,1)=space) do
   if np>length(A(nl))
   then nl:=nl+1; np:=1 else np:=np+1 endif
endwhile

if nl≤n
then ep:=np+1
     while ep≤length(A(nl)) and mid(A(nl),ep,1)≠space do
        ep:=ep+1
     endwhile
     result:=mid(A(nl),np,ep-np)
else result:=empty string
endif
```

It would probably be appropriate to ask the system designer whether or not new values should be assigned to the variables bl and bp, e.g. in preparation for a subsequent call to this subprogram (to find the following name in the array). If so, then the postcondition must be changed and extended accordingly. The additional assignment statements would be bl:=nl and bp:=ep (at the end of the then branch) or bp:=1 (at the end of the else branch).

5.5 SUMMARY: PROGRAM DESIGN

In this chapter four examples illustrated how to design error free programs, using the proof rules as guidelines. In each case we began with the pre- and postconditions – i.e. with the specification of the program to be designed. Before investing time in programming, we determined precisely and clearly what the program should do – in other words, what we wanted to design. For if one does not know what the goal is, then it is unlikely that one will achieve it.

It is always worthwhile to invest time in a clear and complete formulation of the postcondition. Not only does the designer of the program segment in question profit, also every programmer of a call to it benefits from clearly and precisely formulated pre- and postconditions. Such a specification tells him exactly and completely what he must concern himself with and provide for before the call and what he may assume after the return.

When the specification of the program to be designed was clear and precise, we decided upon the basic structure for our program: a loop, an if statement or a sequence of statements. Repetition of an operation suggests a loop; a case distinction in the analysis, an if statement. When the postcondition consists of subexpressions which build upon one another, a sequence of statements is frequently appropriate. In such a sequence each statement (which itself may be compound, i.e. made up of subsidiary statements) establishes the truth of the corresponding subexpression of the postcondition.

After choosing a loop as our basic program structure, we determined the loop invariant by generalizing the pre- and postconditions. Of the two, the postcondition was the more important basis for developing the loop invariant.

We then derived the end condition of the loop from the difference between the loop invariant and the postcondition. To do this, we asked ourselves the questions, "when does the loop invariant also represent the postcondition?" or "under what condition does the loop invariant imply the postcondition?". Finally, the while condition was determined by negating the end condition.

Each time we designed the body of the loop so that it (1) made progress toward fulfilling the postcondition and (2) maintained the truth of the loop invariant. Any other consideration is superfluous when designing the loop body.

The initialization of every loop was designed so that it would establish the truth of the loop invariant. Here, too, any other consideration is superfluous.

As elsewhere, practice makes perfect. It is not difficult to learn the generally applicable approach presented here, but neither is it trivially easy. Software developers who have taken the time and effort to do so report that it definitely paid off. Also the users of their software are pleased with the results.

6

FORMULATING PRE- AND POSTCONDITIONS

6.1 BOOLEAN EXPRESSIONS: A LANGUAGE

Before a program can be proved correct, its pre- and postconditions must be available and in appropriate form – logical algebraic expressions. If the system designer has not provided them, then the designer of the program segment in question must write the pre- and postconditions in this form himself.

Many with little or no experience in proving programs correct find this important step somewhat difficult at first. We will, therefore, concern ourselves with this process in this chapter.

The process of formulating the pre- and postconditions as logical algebraic expressions given a verbal description of the program is, fundamentally, nothing other than translating between two different languages. In this case the target language is a subset of the language of mathematics.

The ability to translate into a particular language presupposes, in general, active knowledge of the target language. This obvious truism also applies when the target language is, as here, the mathematical language. Practice in reading, interpreting and manipulating logical algebraic expressions helps considerably in acquiring the ability to express thoughts, requirements, etc., in this form.

It is suggested, therefore, that the reader view logical (Boolean) algebra as a language. Read logical algebraic expressions frequently, translate them into English and write in this language in order to gain experience, increase your active knowledge and become fluent. Study again, for example, the development of the postconditions in sections 5.1.1, 5.2.1, 5.3.2 and 5.4.2.

The language of Boolean algebra used in this book is based on the logical functions **and, or** and **not**. The implication ($\Longrightarrow$) is a useful, but not absolutely necessary extension. (See the section "Mathematical notation" at the beginning of this book and Appendix A.) The subexpressions which are combined by the logical functions can be formed using other mathematical functions (e.g. <, >, =, +, -, *, /, etc.).

6.2 Translating from English into the Language of Logical Algebra

In order to formulate the pre- and postconditions of a program, given a general description of the effect of its execution, the following approach is often useful. From the description of the *effects* or *changes* caused by the execution of the program, derive descriptions of the *states* prevailing before and after execution. Relationships between the values of the various program variables should constitute the subject of these state descriptions.

Step by step, these descriptions of the states before and after execution of the program are made more precise until they can be written in the form of logical algebraic expressions. Then these expressions are simplified, if possible and appropriate. The results are the desired pre- and postconditions.

It is sometimes advantageous in this translation process to draw diagrams of various types, using them as intermediate descriptive forms. Chapter 5 contains a number of examples of such diagrams. It should be remembered, however, that such diagrams supplement, facilitate interpreting or help to formulate the logical algebraic expressions. The diagrams are *not* substitutes for the algebraic expressions and one should resist any temptation to use them as such.

6.3 Additional Suggestions for Pre- and Postconditions and Loop Invariants

As a general rule, assertions about the ranges of all key variables should be included in the pre- and postconditions. In the precondition, such assertions should normally be as weak (unrestrictive) as possible. In the postcondition, they should generally be as strong (restrictive) as feasible. The postcondition should contain assertions about the ranges of all variables modified by the program segment in question.

Correspondingly, every loop invariant should contain assertions about the ranges of all program variables modified by the loop body. These assertions should be as strong (restrictive) as possible and should include both upper and lower bounds. It is often easier to prove that the loop terminates if these guidelines are followed.

It is usually advisable to write conditions – especially postconditions – in the form

(A1 **and** ...) **or** (A2 **and** ...) **or** ... (An **and** ...)

or, similarly,

...
and [(A1 **and** ...) **or** (A2 **and** ...) **or** ... (An **and** ...)]

where A1, A2, etc., are simple and mutually exclusive conditions. When the postcondition is in this form, tests in the subsequent program segment to distinguish between the several cases are particularly simple. Cf. the postconditions in sections 5.1.1, 5.3.2 and 5.4.2.

6.4 A SMALL GLOSSARY FOR ENGLISH–BOOLEAN ALGEBRA

In the English descriptions of the effects of executing a program or the states before and after execution, certain terms and phrases frequently appear which correspond to particular logical algebraic forms. These can be translated immediately into the target language to form the basis for the rest of the pre- or postcondition.

Frequently appearing verbal terms and phrases correspond to logical functions and algebraic expressions as follows:

English	Boolean algebra
and, but	**and**
or	**or**
(for) all, every	**and** series
(for) no, none	**and** series with negated assertion
there is (are), there exists, (for) some, at least one	**or** series
sorted $[A(1) \le A(2) \le \ldots \le A(n)]$	$\text{and}_{i=1}^{n-1} A(i) \le A(i+1)$
integer, whole number	$\ldots \varepsilon Z$
if (when, whenever) ... then ...	$\Longrightarrow$
search, find, equal, present	$=$
exchange, rearrange, different order (sequence), merge, copy, sort	permutation (see section 6.5)

6.5 EXAMPLES OF TRANSLATING INTO THE LANGUAGE OF LOGICAL ALGEBRA

In several examples in chapter 5 we developed pre- and postconditions from verbal descriptions of the program to be designed. See especially sections 5.1.1, 5.2.1, 5.3.2 and 5.4.2.

Below we will examine still more examples of this translation process.

6.5.1 Merging

Consider the following informal specification of a subprogram which we want to express in logical algebraic form: "The values stored in arrays A and B are merged and stored in array C. Before the subprogram is called, arrays A and B are sorted. Afterward, array C is sorted. The variables na and nb indicate how many elements there are in arrays A and B respectively."

The term "sorted" suggests **and** series in the pre- and post-conditions (see section 6.4). It is not clear whether the ranges of the array subscripts begin with 0, 1 or some other value. We will assume here that they begin with 1. This assumption should be verified with the system designer.

The precondition should express the requirement that the arrays A and B be sorted. It should also include an assertion about the range of the variables na and nb. Only integer values are meaningful. Negative values obviously make no sense. A value of 1 or more must be regarded as normal and, therefore, permitted. If na=0 or nb=0, then the corresponding array is empty. Even though such a case might not be "normal", it would certainly be meaningful. Because a precondition should, in general, be as weak (unrestrictive) as possible, we will allow 0 as a value for na and nb. The precondition becomes:

$$na \epsilon Z \textbf{ and } nb \epsilon Z \textbf{ and } na \geq 0 \textbf{ and } nb \geq 0 \qquad \text{[ranges of na, nb]}$$

$$\textbf{and}_{i=1}^{na-1} A(i) \leq A(i+1) \textbf{ and}_{i=1}^{nb-1} B(i) \leq B(i+1) \text{ [A, B sorted]}$$

The postcondition should assert that the array C is sorted and that the values in array C after execution of the program were copied from the arrays A and B. A corresponding postcondition is as follows:

$$\textbf{and}_{i=1}^{na+nb-1} \; C(i) \le C(i+1) \qquad\qquad \text{[C sorted]}$$

and the sequence {C(1), C(2), ... C(na+nb)} is a permutation of the sequence {A(1), ... A(na), B(1), ... B(nb)}

[values in C copied from A and B]

The last term in the postcondition states that the values in array C are the same as those in arrays A and B. Only the order may be different. This term eliminates the possibility that array C contains values differing from those in arrays A and B.

A permutation of a sequence is a rearrangement of its members (terms). Two sequences are permutations of each other if they differ only in the order of their terms. If a particular value appears in a sequence several times, then that value must appear the same number of times in a permutation of the sequence.

6.5.2 Sorting

Consider the following informal specification of a subprogram which we want to express in logical algebraic form: "The array X is given. The integer subscript ranges from il to ir inclusive. The array may be empty. The program to be designed should sort the values in array X by rearranging (permuting) them appropriately."

The precondition must express the relationship between the values of the variables il and ir arising from the fact that the number of elements in array X is 0 or positive: $ir-il+1 \ge 0$. Equivalent and perhaps clearer is the form $il-1 \le ir$. Adding the assertion that the values of il and ir must be integers, our precondition becomes

$il \varepsilon Z$ **and** $ir \varepsilon Z$ **and** $il-1 \le ir$

What state should prevail after execution of the program? The values in array X should be in order (sorted). The informal specification does not state whether ascending or descending sequence is desired; we will assume that they should be sorted into ascending sequence with equal values allowed. Furthermore, these values should be the same as the ones in array X before the program was executed, although they may be in different places within the array afterward. Translated into the language of logical algebra, our postcondition is

$$\text{\textbf{and}}_{i=il}^{ir-1} \; X(i) \le X(i+1) \qquad\qquad \text{[X sorted]}$$

and the sequence {X(il), X(il+1), ... X(ir)} is a permutation
of the sequence {X'(il), X'(il+1), ... X'(ir)}

[values in X originally in X]

The apostrophe (') here refers to the value of the corresponding array variable *before* execution of the sorting program being designed.

6.5.3 Qualified (conditional) conditions

In a pre- or postcondition we must sometimes require a certain condition B to be fulfilled, but only if some other condition A is true. When A is not true (false), then it does not matter whether B is fulfilled (true) or not. Such a qualified (conditional) requirement is often **and**ed with other conditions in the pre- or postcondition. For a requirement of this type the logical implication

A $\Longrightarrow$ B

is appropriate. This implication is equivalent to (see Appendix A, section A.3, identity 22)

not A **or** B

In the latter expression it is especially clear that the value of B is immaterial when A is false. When A is true, this expression simplifies to the condition B.

Example: Consider a subprogram which merges values from presorted arrays A and B into array C, which must also be sorted. The loop invariant must include the requirement that the next element to be copied from array A (A(ia)) be greater than or equal to the last element in array C (C(ic-1)), but only if there is another element in array A to be copied (ia$\le$na) and array C already contains an element (ic>1). The corresponding "conditional" condition is ia≤na **and** ic>1 ⟹ C(ic-1)≤A(ia)

This implication is equivalent to the expression

ia>na **or** ic≤1 **or** C(ic-1)≤A(ia)

which can be read (interpreted, translated into English) as follows: The requirement is fulfilled when either

• there is no element left in array A to be copied or

• no element has as yet been copied to array C (array C is empty) or

• the last element in array C is less than or equal to the next element in array A.

The corresponding condition must be placed on the next element of array B also:

ib≤nb **and** ic>1 ⟹ C(ic-1)≤B(ib)

See also section 4.5 above. ■

6.6 SUMMARY: FORMULATING LOGICAL ALGEBRAIC CONDITIONS

Formulating pre- and postconditions based on given informal verbal descriptions of the effects of executing a program is a translation process. Therefore, active knowledge of the target language − a subset of the language of mathematics − is a prerequisite for the ability to write pre- and postconditions in the necessary form, i.e. as logical algebraic expressions. In order to become sufficiently fluent in logical (Boolean) algebra, one must invest a certain − but not especially large − amount of time and effort learning this material.

7

CONCLUSION

7.1 THE THEORETICAL FOUNDATION FOR ERROR FREE SOFTWARE IN PRACTICE

In the last one to two decades a mathematical and theoretical foundation has been developed for designing provably correct software. The nature of this foundation, the way in which it can be applied to practical software design problems and the quality of the resulting software – in particular freedom from design errors – exhibit great similarity to the corresponding aspects of the classical engineering fields. This mathematical and theoretical foundation is a primary and essential prerequisite for a truly engineering approach to software development.

The subject of this book is the practical application of the foundation mentioned above, not the theory itself. We have learned the most essential aspects of this material in the form of proof rules. The proof rules are applied directly in order to verify a correctness proposition (consisting of a precondition, a program or program segment and a postcondition) and to derive a precondition for a given program and a given postcondition.

When verifying a correctness proposition, one applies the proof rules in order to decompose the original correctness proposition into correctness propositions about the component parts of the program in a way corresponding to the structure of the original program. This process is repeated iteratively until only correctness propositions about assignment statements and already proved propositions (e.g. about subprograms) remain. Correctness propositions about assignment statements are verified directly by applying suitable proof rules.

By organizing a program as a hierarchical structure of subprograms, each of limited size, and by decomposing the proof into corresponding subproofs (lemmas), it is feasible in practice to prove even a large program correct.

Even more importantly for software development practice, useful guidelines for designing a program can be derived from the proof rules and their application. These guidelines direct the designer's attention to the important and essential aspects of the program and away from its unimportant and inessential aspects. The software developer works more systematically and goal oriented than in the traditional way. Typically the result is a more compact program which is logically simpler and correspondingly easier to understand. Often several parts of the program can be derived directly. The proof of correctness (or at least a detailed sketch thereof) is developed simultaneously with the program, as a by-product. (Some would take the opposite standpoint: the program is developed as a by-product of constructing the proof.)

The methods and approach presented in this book enable the software developer to verify that his program design satisfies the requirements (the specification) – before running or "testing" it – just as engineers in the classical fields do. In particular, he can determine under what conditions the program will reliably yield correct results, i.e., when one may have confidence in the results (and when not). Without such knowledge and information, he cannot assume the same type of responsibility for the program that his engineering colleagues regularly do for their designs.

This book is concerned only with logical algebraic expressions (e.g. pre- and postconditions) which refer to the *values* of program variables. Such expressions are the most important of those arising in practice and cover the most essential and problematic aspects of program logic and correctness. Other types of assertions, e.g. about the structure of data environments, are treated in the scientific literature [Baber, 1987]. The professional software developer will find it worthwhile to study the theory underlying the material presented in this book in order to extend his knowledge to include such more advanced topics (see the Bibliography).

7.2 SOFTWARE DEVELOPMENT TOMORROW

It was already mentioned in section 1.1 that computer systems are being employed in an ever widening range of application areas in our society. The number of applications requiring very high levels of reliability (e.g. safety critical systems upon which human lives depend) will grow significantly. It will become ever more important that software embedded in such systems be free of design errors. The developers of such software will be held increasingly responsible for their programs – and above all, for their mistakes.

In the middle to long term, software development will be placed on a proper engineering basis, for really reliable software is not only possible but also sorely needed. In the future practice of software development, a very different mentality will prevail – both technically and with regard to responsibility for the correctness (freedom from design errors) of programs. The software developer will be expected to "calculate" the behaviour of his program analytically and systematically, thereby proving that it is consistent with the specification – much as the structural engineer calculates the statics of the object he is designing. The software developer of the future will fulfill this expectation. An approach enabling him to do so was presented in this book.

Software developers of today should begin as soon as possible to prepare themselves for the software development world of tomorrow, which will be quite different from the software development world to which they are now accustomed. For developing in the traditional way software upon which human life depends is nothing other than high tech Russian roulette.

APPENDIX A. LOGICAL (BOOLEAN) ALGEBRA

In the following sections, x, y and z are variables or expressions whose values are false or true.

A.1 DEFINITIONS OF THE BOOLEAN FUNCTIONS

The Boolean functions **and, or,** implication ($\Longrightarrow$) and **not** are defined in the following truth tables:

x	y	x **and** y	x **or** y	x $\Longrightarrow$ y
false	false	false	false	true
false	true	false	true	true
true	false	false	true	false
true	true	true	true	true

x	not x
false	true
true	false

A.2 ORDER OF EVALUATING FUNCTIONS IN EXPRESSIONS

The various functions appearing in an expression are typically evaluated in the following order, unless indicated otherwise by parentheses.

↑ (exponentiation)
+, - (sign)
*, / (multiplication, division)
+, - (addition, subtraction)
<, >, =, ≤, ≥, ≠ (relational functions)
not (also written ¬)
and (also written ∧)
or (also written ∨)
⟹ (logical implication)

A.3 FUNDAMENTAL PROPERTIES
OF THE BOOLEAN FUNCTIONS

The following relationships (mostly equations) express particularly important properties of the Boolean functions. They are applied often when manipulating and simplifying logical algebraic expressions; use this list, therefore, as a reference.

It is recommended that the reader verify the equations and other formulas below as an exercise. Use the definitions given in section A.1 above as a starting point.

The functions **and** and **or** are commutative:

1. (x **and** y) = (y **and** x)
2. (x **or** y) = (y **or** x)

The functions **and** and **or** are associative:

    3. (x **and** (y **and** z)) = ((x **and** y) **and** z)
    4. (x **or** (y **or** z)) = ((x **or** y) **or** z)

The functions **and** and **or** are distributive:

    5. (x **and** (y **or** z)) = ((x **and** y) **or** (x **and** z))
    6. (x **or** (y **and** z)) = ((x **or** y) **and** (x **or** z))

Simple identities:

    7. (x **and** **not** x) = false
    8. (x **and** false) = false
    9. (x **and** x) = x
  10. (x **and** true) = x

  11. (x **or** false) = x
  12. (x **or** x) = x
  13. (x **or** true) = true
  14. (x **or** **not** x) = true

  15. (**not** (**not** x)) = x

Additional identities:

  16. (x **or** (x **and** y)) = x
  17. (x **or** (**not** x **and** y)) = (x **or** y)
  18. ((x **or** y) **and** (x **or** z)) = (x **or** y **and** z)

The negation of **and** and **or** expressions:

  19. (**not** (x **and** y)) = ((**not** x) **or** (**not** y))
  20. (**not** (x **or** y)) = ((**not** x) **and** (**not** y))

Alternative expressions for the implication:

  21. (x ⟹ y) = (**not** (x **and** **not** y))
  22. (x ⟹ y) = ((**not** x) **or** y)
  23. (x ⟹ y) = ((**not** y) ⟹ (**not** x))
  24. (z **and** (x ⟹ y)) = (z **and** ((z **and** x) ⟹ y))

Alternative expression for equality:

  25. (x = y) = ((x **and** y) **or** (**not** x **and** **not** y))

    Notice that (x **and** y) = (x **and** z) provided only that y=z when x is true. When x is false, (x **and** y) = (x **and** z) regardless of whether y=z or not. Symbolically,

    26. $[x \implies (y=z)] \implies [(x$ **and** $y) = (x$ **and** $z)]$

A.4 Exercises in Logical Algebra

1. Let B, C and D be Boolean variables or expressions. The new function F is defined as follows:

    F = C, if B=true,
       = D, if B=false

Write an equivalent expression for F. Use only B, C, D and the Boolean functions **and, or** and **not**. Show that your new expression satisfies the above definition of F.

2. Strengthening and weakening conditions: Show that the following statements are true for all values of x and y.

    x **and** y $\implies$ x
    x $\implies$ x **or** y

3. Show that the following expressions are equal:

    x **and** (y **or** z)
    x **and** (x **and** y **or** z)
    x **and** (y **or** x **and** z)
    x **and** (x **and** y **or** x **and** z)
    x **and** y **or** x **and** z

4. Show that the following is true: If

    a $\implies$ x **and**
    b $\implies$ y

then

    a **and** b $\implies$ x **and** y **and**
    a **or** b $\implies$ x **or** y

5. Simplify or expand the following expressions:

    1. x **and** (y $\implies$ z)
    2. x **or** (y $\implies$ z)
    3. (x **and** y) $\implies$ z
    4. (x **or** y) $\implies$ z

5. $-a > 0$ **and** $a < 0$ **or** $a > 0$ **and** **not** $a < 0$
6. $-a \geq 0$ **and** $a < 0$ **or** $a \geq 0$ **and** **not** $a < 0$
7. $-a < 0$ **and** $a < 0$ **or** $a < 0$ **and** **not** $a < 0$
8. $-a \leq 0$ **and** $a < 0$ **or** $a \leq 0$ **and** **not** $a < 0$

A.5 THE **AND** AND **OR** SERIES

The **and** and **or** series are defined as follows:

$$\textbf{and}_{i=1}^{n} A(i) \equiv A(1) \textbf{ and } A(2) \ldots \textbf{ and } A(n)$$

$$\textbf{or}_{i=1}^{n} A(i) \equiv A(1) \textbf{ or } A(2) \ldots \textbf{ or } A(n)$$

where $A(i)$ is any expression in which the variable i may appear. The variable i is not a program variable, but rather a *running variable* for the series; outside the series it has no meaning.

The value of an empty **and** series ($n < 1$ above) is by definition true; the value of an empty **or** series, false. (Cf. the Σ and Π notation for sums and products.)

It is obvious that

$$[\textbf{and}_{i=1}^{n} A(i)] = [A(n) \textbf{ and}_{i=1}^{n-1} A(i)]$$

if $n \geq 1$. However, a term can be taken out of a series only when the original series contains at least one term. In general (i.e., when the original series may be empty) the following applies:

$$[\textbf{and}_{i=1}^{n} A(i)] = [n < 1 \textbf{ or } n \geq 1 \textbf{ and } A(n) \textbf{ and}_{i=1}^{n-1} A(i)]$$

For the **or** series the corresponding formula is

$$[\textbf{or}_{i=1}^{n} A(i)] = [n \geq 1 \textbf{ and } (A(n) \textbf{ or}_{i=1}^{n-1} A(i))]$$

Exercise:

1. Verify the identities above. Hint:

$$[\textbf{and}_{i=1}^{n} A(i)] = [(n < 1 \textbf{ or } n \geq 1) \textbf{ and}_{i=1}^{n} A(i)] \;\blacksquare$$

APPENDIX B. SOLUTIONS TO THE EXERCISES

The problem numbers shown below are made up of the number of the section in which the exercise appears and the number of the problem within the exercise.

4.1.1 (1). $\{0 \le i\}$ i:=i+1 $\{1 \le i\}$

4.1.1 (2). $\{sum+z=x+y+z\}$ sum:=sum+z $\{sum=x+y+z\}$. Often the precondition can be simplified to $\{sum=x+y\}$. However, if the addition symbol (+) in the assignment statement refers to floating point arithmetic, then one must remember that (1) this simplification assumes that addition is associative $[(...+z)-z = ...+(z-z)]$, a requirement not generally satisfied by floating point addition, and that (2) the addition symbol (+) in the postcondition may refer to standard mathematical addition, which is not the same operation as floating point addition. In the latter case, one should use two different symbols for the two different addition operations.

4.1.1 (3). $\{w*y - 2*w^2 < z\}$ x:=5-z $\{w*y - 2*w^2 < z\}$. The variable x does not appear in the postcondition. By proof rule A1, the postcondition is also the precondition in this case.

4.2 (1). $\{x\neq 0\}$ if x<0 then y:=-x else y:=x endif $\{y>0\}$. Apply proof rule IF2. V1 = $\{-x>0\}$ = $\{x<0\}$, V2 = $\{x>0\}$, B = $\{x<0\}$, not B = $\{x\geq 0\}$.

4.2 (2). $\{$true$\}$ if x<0 then y:=-x else y:=x endif $\{y\geq 0\}$. The precondition is the logical constant true. The postcondition will always be satisfied (true) after execution of the if statement.

4.2 (3). $\{$false$\}$ if x<0 then y:=-x else y:=x endif $\{y<0\}$. The precondition is the logical constant false. The postcondition will never be satisfied after execution of the if statement.

4.2 (4). $\{x=0\}$ if x<0 then y:=-x else y:=x endif $\{y\leq 0\}$

4.2 (5). $\{3\leq |x|\leq 4\}$ if x<0 then y:=-x else y:=x endif $\{2\leq y\leq 4\}$ is true. Apply proof rules IF1 and A2. Alternatively, the application of proof rule IF2 yields $\{2\leq |x|\leq 4\}$ as a precondition. By proof rule P1, the stronger given precondition is also a precondition.

4.3 (1). We apply proof rules S1 and A1. Beginning with the postcondition and the last assignment statement, we work backwards to the beginning of the sequence of statements. (Read, therefore, from bottom to top.)

$\{0\leq N\}$

=

$\{(0>M-N$ **or** $0\leq M-N)$ **and** $0\leq N\}$

i:=0

$\{(0>M-N$ **or** $0\leq M-N$ **and** $_{a=0}{}^{i-1}$ D(0+a)=K(a)) **and** $0\leq i\leq N\}$

j:=0

$\{$**and**$_{k=0}{}^{j-1}$ (**not and**$_{a=0}{}^{N-1}$ D(k+a)=K(a))

and $(j>M-N$ **or** $j\leq M-N$ **and**$_{a=0}{}^{i-1}$ D(j+a)=K(a))

and $0\leq j$ **and** $0\leq i\leq N\}$

4.5 (1). The following two correctness propositions are to be verified (see section 4.5):

{I **and** ia≤na **and** (ib>nb **or** A(ia)≤B(ib))}
C(ic):=A(ia)
ia:=ia+1
{I$^{ic}_{ic+1}$}

and

{I **and** ib≤nb **and** (ia>na **or** B(ib)<A(ia))}
C(ic):=B(ib)
ib:=ib+1
{I$^{ic}_{ic+1}$}

By proof rule P1, the last proposition above will be true if

{I **and** ib≤nb **and** (ia>na **or** B(ib)≤A(ia))}
C(ic):=B(ib)
ib:=ib+1
{I$^{ic}_{ic+1}$}

Now the two correctness propositions to be proved (the first and the last above) are completely symmetric in A/a and B/b. (The loop invariant I is symmetric.)

4.5 (2). The following correctness propositions are to be verified (see 4.5 (1) above):

{I **and** ia≤na **and** (ib>nb **or** A(ia)≤B(ib))}
C(ic):=A(ia)
ia:=ia+1
{In$^{ic}_{ic+1}$}

and

{I **and** ib≤nb **and** (ia>na **or** B(ib)≤A(ia))}
C(ic):=B(ib)
ib:=ib+1
{In$^{ic}_{ic+1}$}

for the seven postconditions

$I1^{ic}_{ic+1}:$ $1 \leq ia \leq na+1$

$I2^{ic}_{ic+1}:$ $1 \leq ib \leq nb+1$

$I3^{ic}_{ic+1}:$ $ic=(ia-1)+(ib-1)$

$I4^{ic}_{ic+1}:$ $(ic \leq 0$ **or** $ia > na$ **or** $C(ic) \leq A(ia))$

$I5^{ic}_{ic+1}:$ $(ic \leq 0$ **or** $ib > nb$ **or** $C(ic) \leq B(ib))$

$I6^{ic}_{ic+1}:$ **and**$_{i=1}^{ic-1}$ $C(i) \leq C(i+1)$

$I7^{ic}_{ic+1}:$ **and**$_{i=1}^{na-1}$ $A(i) \leq A(i+1)$ **and**$_{i=1}^{nb-1}$ $B(i) \leq B(i+1)$

4.5 (3). Because of the symmetry between A/a and B/b, we need prove only the seven correctness propositions

> {I **and** $ia \leq na$ **and** $(ib > nb$ **or** $A(ia) \leq B(ib))$}
> $C(ic):=A(ia)$
> $ia:=ia+1$
> {In^{ic}_{ic+1}}

for n=1, 2, ... 7. For each postcondition we derive a precondition with respect to the sequence of the two assignment statements by applying proof rules A1 and S1. Then, we verify that the derived precondition follows from the one given above (applying proof rule P1). In the trivial cases 2 and 7, the precondition is the same as the postcondition and it follows directly from the loop invariant I. For the other cases we derive the preconditions:

1: {$0 \leq ia \leq na$} $C(ic):=A(ia)$; $ia:=ia+1$ {$1 \leq ia \leq na+1$}

3: {$ic=ia+(ib-1)$} $C(ic):=A(ia)$; $ia:=ia+1$ {$ic=(ia-1)+(ib-1)$}

4: {$ic \leq 0$ **or** $ia+1 > na$ **or** $A(ia) \leq A(ia+1)$}
     $C(ic):=A(ia)$; $ia:=ia+1$
     {$ic \leq 0$ **or** $ia > na$ **or** $C(ic) \leq A(ia)$}

5: $\{ic \leq 0$ **or** $ib > nb$ **or** $A(ia) \leq B(ib)\}$
   $C(ic) := A(ia); \; ia := ia+1$
   $\{ic \leq 0$ **or** $ib > nb$ **or** $C(ic) \leq B(ib)\}$

6: $\{ic \leq 1$ **or** $C(ic-1) \leq A(ia)$ **and**$_{i=1}^{ic-2} \; C(i) \leq C(i+1)\}$

   $C(ic) := A(ia); \; ia := ia+1 \; \{$**and**$_{i=1}^{ic-1} \; C(i) \leq C(i+1)\}$

We must still show that these derived preconditions follow from the given precondition (cf. proof rules P1 and A2).

1: The given precondition contains (I **and** $ia \leq na$), which implies $1 \leq ia \leq na$. This, in turn, implies the derived precondition $0 \leq ia \leq na$.

3: The derived precondition is equivalent to the expression $(ic-1) = (ia-1) + (ib-1)$, one of the **and**ed terms in the loop invariant I and hence in the given precondition.

4: The loop invariant I implies that $ic \geq 1$ (see I1, I2 and I3). Thus the term $ic \leq 0$ in the derived precondition will always be false. The rest of the derived precondition is equivalent to $[ia \leq na-1 \implies A(ia) \leq A(ia+1)]$. This condition follows from I7 in combination with I1. The given precondition implies, therefore, the derived precondition. Formally,

   $\{$I **and** $ia \leq na$ **and** $(ib > nb$ **or** $A(ia) \leq B(ib))\}$
   $\implies$
   I
   $\implies$
   I1 **and** I7
   $\implies$
   $1 \leq ia$ **and**$_{i=1}^{na-1} \; A(i) \leq A(i+1)$
   $\implies$
   $1 \leq ia$ **and** $(1 \leq ia \leq na-1 \implies A(ia) \leq A(ia+1))$
   $=$ [see Appendix A, section A.3, identity 24]
   $1 \leq ia$ **and** $(ia \leq na-1 \implies A(ia) \leq A(ia+1))$
   $\implies$
   $(ia \leq na-1 \implies A(ia) \leq A(ia+1))$
   $=$
   $ia > na-1$ **or** $A(ia) \leq A(ia+1)$
   $=$
   $ia+1 > na$ **or** $A(ia) \leq A(ia+1)$
   $\implies$

ic≤0 **or** ia+1>na **or** A(ia)≤A(ia+1)

5: The first term will always be false (see 4 above). The rest of the derived precondition is an **and**ed term in the given precondition and therefore follows from it.

6: The derived precondition follows from (I **and** ia≤na), part of the given precondition. In particular, the derived precondition follows from (I4 **and** ia≤na **and** I6).

5.2.10 (1). In order to derive a precondition with respect to the exchange statement x:=:y, simultaneously replace x by y and y by x everywhere in the postcondition. Alternatively, one can replace the exchange statement by the equivalent sequence of assignment statements

auxvar:=y; y:=x; x:=auxvar

and prove the resulting program correct. Care must be taken that this use of the auxiliary variable auxvar does not interfere with the other effects of the program. In particular, the variable auxvar may not appear in the postcondition of the exchange statement.

5.2.10 (2). The following correctness proposition about the entire program segment is to be verified:

```
{il≤ir}
gl:=il; gr:=gl; k:=ir
while gr<k do
    if X(gr+1)<X(gl)
    then X(gl):=:X(gr+1)
         gl:=gl+1; gr:=gr+1
    else if X(gr+1)=X(gl)
    then gr:=gr+1
    else [Remark: X(gr+1)>X(gl)]
         X(k):=:X(gr+1)
         k:=k-1
    endif
    endif
endwhile
```

$$\{il \le gl \le gr \le ir \text{ and}_{i=il}^{gl-1} X(i) < X(gl)$$

$$\text{and}_{i=gl}^{gr} X(i) = X(gl) \text{ and}_{i=gr+1}^{ir} X(i) > X(gl)\}$$

The loop invariant I is known from the design phase:

$$il \leq gl \leq gr \leq k \leq ir \text{ and}_{i=il}^{gl-1} X(i) < X(gl)$$

$$\text{and}_{i=gl}^{gr} X(i) = X(gl) \text{ and}_{i=k+1}^{ir} X(i) > X(gl)$$

It was already proved in section 5.2.9 that the loop terminates. Therefore, we will prove only partial correctness here.

By applying proof rule W2, we decompose the correctness proposition above into the following three correctness propositions which we must verify.

$\{il \leq ir\}$ gl:=il; gr:=gl; k:=ir $\{I\}$ [1]

$\{I$ **and** $gr<k\}$ **if** ... **endif** $\{I\}$ [2]

$\{I$ **and not** $gr<k\}$ [3]
$\Longrightarrow$

$$\{il \leq gl \leq gr \leq ir \text{ and}_{i=il}^{gl-1} X(i) < X(gl)$$

$$\text{and}_{i=gl}^{gr} X(i) = X(gl) \text{ and}_{i=gr+1}^{ir} X(i) > X(gl)\}$$

Proposition 1 above was, in effect, verified already in section 5.2.8, where we derived the precondition by applying proof rules A1 and S1.

The proof of proposition 3 above is straightforward and relatively simple. $\{I$ **and not** $gr<k\} = \{I$ **and** $gr \geq k\} \Longrightarrow gr=k$. Replace k by gr in the loop invariant; the result is the postcondition.

Proposition 2 above can be decomposed by applying proof rule IF1. Three correctness propositions about the individual branches of the if statement result. Fully written out, they are as follows:

$$\{il \leq gl \leq gr < k \leq ir \text{ and}_{i=il}^{gl-1} X(i) < X(gl) \qquad [2.1]$$

$$\text{and}_{i=gl}^{gr} X(i) = X(gl) \text{ and}_{i=k+1}^{ir} X(i) > X(gl)$$

$$\text{and } X(gr+1) < X(gl)\}$$

$$X(gl) :=: X(gr+1); \quad gl := gl+1; \quad gr := gr+1$$

$$\{il \leq gl \leq gr \leq k \leq ir \text{ and}_{i=il}^{gl-1} X(i) < X(gl)$$

$$\text{and}_{i=gl}^{gr} X(i) = X(gl) \text{ and}_{i=k+1}^{ir} X(i) > X(gl)\}$$

and

$$\{il \leq gl \leq gr < k \leq ir \text{ and}_{i=il}^{gl-1} X(i) < X(gl) \qquad [2.2]$$

$$\text{and}_{i=gl}^{gr} X(i) = X(gl) \text{ and}_{i=k+1}^{ir} X(i) > X(gl)$$

$$\text{and } X(gr+1) = X(gl)\}$$

$$gr := gr+1$$

$$\{il \leq gl \leq gr \leq k \leq ir \text{ and}_{i=il}^{gl-1} X(i) < X(gl)$$

$$\text{and}_{i=gl}^{gr} X(i) = X(gl) \text{ and}_{i=k+1}^{ir} X(i) > X(gl)\}$$

and

$$\{il \leq gl \leq gr < k \leq ir \text{ and}_{i=il}^{gl-1} X(i) < X(gl) \qquad [2.3]$$

$$\text{and}_{i=gl}^{gr} X(i) = X(gl) \text{ and}_{i=k+1}^{ir} X(i) > X(gl)$$

$$\text{and } X(gr+1) > X(gl)\}$$

$$X(k) :=: X(gr+1); \quad k := k-1$$

$$\{il \leq gl \leq gr \leq k \leq ir \text{ and}_{i=il}^{gl-1} X(i) < X(gl)$$

$$\text{and}_{i=gl}^{gr} X(i) = X(gl) \text{ and}_{i=k+1}^{ir} X(i) > X(gl)\}$$

The above propositions are proved by applying proof rules A1, A2 and S1. First a precondition of the loop invariant (as postcondition) with respect to the sequence of assignment statements is derived. Then we verify that the given precondition implies the derived precondition.

Correctness proposition 2.2 above relates to a single assignment to a simple (not indexed) variable. Its proof is correspondingly short and straightforward. Proposition 2.1 relates to the longest sequence of statements and its proof is the most complex. Furthermore, the algebraic manipulation in its proof can be greatly facilitated by a particularly suitable, but simple transformation of the postcondition and an appropriate application of proof rule P1. Therefore, we will prove proposition 2.1 in detail.

In the first step, we replace gr and gl by gr+1 and gl+1 respectively in the postcondition. This will give rise to references to X(gl+1). Then we must replace references to X(gr+1). Depending upon whether gl+1=gr+1 or not, the references to X(gl+1) should or should not be replaced. This dependence would complicate the algebraic manipulation at that point considerably; it would be much more convenient if such references should be either unconditionally replaced or unconditionally not replaced.

The postcondition implies that X(gl)=X(gr) (see the **and** series for the = region). If we rewrite the postcondition accordingly, the references in question will be limited to X(gr+1), which should be replaced unconditionally. The new expression for the postcondition is

$$\{il \leq gl \leq gr \leq k \leq ir \ \textbf{and}_{i=il}^{gl-1} \ X(i) < X(gr)$$

$$\textbf{and}_{i=gl}^{gr} \ X(i) = X(gr) \ \textbf{and}_{i=k+1}^{ir} \ X(i) > X(gr)\}$$

The precondition with respect to the sequence of the last two assignment statements (gl:=gl+1; gr:=gr+1) is

$$\{il \leq gl+1 \leq gr+1 \leq k \leq ir \ \textbf{and}_{i=il}^{gl} \ X(i) < X(gr+1)$$

$$\textbf{and}_{i=gl+1}^{gr+1} \ X(i) = X(gr+1) \ \textbf{and}_{i=k+1}^{ir} \ X(i) > X(gr+1)\}$$

The first term is equivalent to (il≤gl+1 **and** gl≤gr<k≤ir). The given precondition ensures that the stronger restriction il≤gl is satisfied. The exchange statement does not affect these variables, so il≤gl will still hold after its execution. Proof rule P1 permits us to strengthen the precondition derived above accordingly to obtain

$$\{il{\leq}gl{\leq}gr{<}k{\leq}ir \text{ and}_{i=il}^{gl} X(i){<}X(gr{+}1)$$

$$\text{and}_{i=gl+1}^{gr+1} X(i){=}X(gr{+}1) \text{ and}_{i=k+1}^{ir} X(i){>}X(gr{+}1)\}$$

as a precondition with respect to the sequence of assignment statements (gl:=gl+1; gr:=gr+1).

Now we must replace X(gl) and X(gr+1) in order to derive a precondition with respect to the exchange statement and the entire sequence of statements. We know that gl≤gr<gr+1. Some of the X(i) are references to X(gl) or X(gr+1); we must separate such references from the others. We must take one term (i=gl) out of the first **and** series. Similarly, we must take one term (i=gr+1) out of the second **and** series. This term is a tautology, thus true, and can therefore be dropped (see Appendix A, section A.3, identity 10).

Our precondition with respect to the sequence of the last two assignment statements, which is also the postcondition for the exchange statement, then becomes

$$\{il{\leq}gl{\leq}gr{<}k{\leq}ir \text{ and}_{i=il}^{gl-1} X(i){<}X(gr{+}1) \text{ and } X(gl){<}X(gr{+}1)$$

$$\text{and}_{i=gl+1}^{gr} X(i){=}X(gr{+}1) \text{ and}_{i=k+1}^{ir} X(i){>}X(gr{+}1)\}$$

Now no X(i) is a reference to either X(gl) or X(gr+1). In the first **and** series, i<gl<gr+1. In the second **and** series, gl<i<gr+1. In the third **and** series, gl<gr+1<k+1≤i, thus gl<gr+1<i (see the first term in the expression above).

Now we can simultaneously replace X(gl) by X(gr+1) and X(gr+1) by X(gl) in order to derive a precondition with respect to the entire branch of the if statement:

$$\{il{\leq}gl{\leq}gr{<}k{\leq}ir \text{ and}_{i=il}^{gl-1} X(i){<}X(gl) \text{ and } X(gr{+}1){<}X(gl)$$

$$\text{and}_{i=gl+1}^{gr} X(i){=}X(gl) \text{ and}_{i=k+1}^{ir} X(i){>}X(gl)\}$$

This derived precondition is equivalent to the given precondition. The term $X(i)=X(gl)$ for $i=gl$ is missing in the second **and** series; this term is clearly true and can, therefore, be **and**ed to the expression. Except for the order of the terms, the derived and given preconditions are otherwise identical.

The proof of proposition 2.3 above is structurally similar, but significantly simpler.

5.3.7 (1). If $N=0$, then the search key K is the empty string (also called the null string). In this case, the program "finds" the empty string at the beginning of the string D (also when D is the empty string) and ends immediately with $j=0$. When $M=0$, then D (the string in which K is being sought) is the empty string. A non-empty string K cannot be present in an empty string D. In this case ($N>0$, $M=0$), the program ends (without executing the body of the loop) with $j=0>M-N=-N$, i.e. with the result "not present". See the postcondition in section 5.3.2.

5.3.7 (2). The case $M<0$ can be interpreted as $M=0$ (see problem 5.3.7. (1)) with the exception that even an empty string K is "not present". The program ends without executing the loop body with $j=0$. However, negative values of M as the length of D have no meaning; therefore they were excluded in the given precondition.

5.3.7 (3). Hint: Distinguish between the two cases $a \leq b$ and $a > b$.

5.3.7 (4). The task is to verify the following correctness proposition about the entire subprogram:

$\{M \epsilon Z$ **and** $0 \leq M$ **and** $N \epsilon Z$ **and** $0 \leq N\}$

```
i:=0; j:=0
while i<N and j≤M-N do
    if D(j+i)=K(i) then i:=i+1 else j:=j+1; i:=0 endif
endwhile
```

$\{j \epsilon Z$ **and** $0 \leq j \leq \max(0, M-N+1)$

and $_{k=0}^{j-1}$ (**or** $_{a=0}^{N-1}$ $D(k+a) \neq K(a))$

and $(j>M-N$ **or** $j \leq M-N$ **and** $_{a=0}^{N-1}$ $D(j+a)=K(a))\}$

By applying proof rule W2, we decompose the correctness proposition above into the following two correctness propositions about smaller program segments and one implication. The loop invariant I was developed in the design step described in section 5.3.3.

$\{M \varepsilon Z$ and $0 \leq M$ and $N \varepsilon Z$ and $0 \leq N\}$ i:=0; j:=0 $\{I\}$ [1]

$\{I$ and $i < N$ and $j \leq M-N\}$ [2]
if $D(j+i)=K(i)$ then i:=i+1 else j:=j+1; i:=0 endif $\{I\}$

$\{I$ and not $(i < N$ and $j \leq M-N)\}$ [3]
$\Longrightarrow$
$\{j \varepsilon Z$ and $0 \leq j \leq \max(0, M-N+1)$

and$_{k=0}^{j-1}$ (or$_{a=0}^{N-1}$ $D(k+a) \neq K(a))$

and $(j > M-N$ or $j \leq M-N$ and$_{a=0}^{N-1}$ $D(j+a)=K(a))\}$

Proposition 1 above was proved in section 5.3.7. The proof of proposition 3 is only an exercise in the manipulation of logical expressions. By applying proof rule IF1, we decompose proposition 2 into correctness propositions about the individual branches of the if statement:

$\{I$ and $i < N$ and $j \leq M-N$ and $D(j+i)=K(i)\}$ [2.1]
i:=i+1 $\{I\}$

$\{I$ and $i < N$ and $j \leq M-N$ and $D(j+i) \neq K(i)\}$ [2.2]
j:=j+1; i:=0 $\{I\}$

Propositions 2.1 and 2.2 can be verified in the usual manner by applying proof rules A1, A2 and S1. At one point in the proof of proposition 2.2 the fact that

$0 \leq i < N$ and $D(j+i) \neq K(i) \Longrightarrow$ or$_{a=0}^{N-1}$ $D(j+a) \neq K(a)$

must be used. (Cf. Appendix A, section A.4, problem 2, second part.)

In addition, we must show that the loop terminates. It is apparent that every execution of the loop body increases either i or j by 1, and that j is never decreased. Because both i and j have upper bounds (see the while condition), the loop must terminate. More formally, define $(j*N+i)$ as the loop variant.

The then branch of the if statement increases the value of this expression by 1. The else branch increases this value by N and decreases it by i (at most N-1); thus on balance, the value of the loop variant is increased by at least 1. The value of the loop variant will, therefore, reach its maximum, which follows from the while condition, after a limited number of executions of the loop body. Then the loop terminates.

5.4.2 (1). The postcondition must be extended by **and**ing the following expression to it:

$1 \leq nl \leq n+1$ [range of nl]

and {nl=n+1 **and** np=1 [range of np, no name]

or nl≤n **and** $1 \leq np < ep \leq length(A(nl))+1$}
[ranges of np, ep, name located]

5.4.2 (2). empty(z1,p1,z2,p2): The region from position (line z1, position p1) until just before position (z2,p2) contains only spaces and line breaks if

$$z1=z2 \text{ and} \quad {}_{p=p1}^{p2-1} \text{ mid}(A(z1),p,1)=\text{space} \qquad \text{[only one line]}$$

or

$$z1 < z2 \qquad\qquad\qquad\qquad\qquad \text{[more than one line]}$$

$$\text{and}_{p=p1}^{\quad length(A(z1))} \text{ mid}(A(z1),p,1)=\text{space} \qquad \text{[line z1]}$$

$$\text{and}_{z=z1+1}^{\quad z2-1} \text{ and}_{p=1}^{\quad length(A(z))} \text{ mid}(A(z),p,1)=\text{space}$$
$$\text{[intermediate lines (if any)]}$$

$$\text{and}_{p=1}^{\quad p2-1} \text{ mid}(A(z2),p,1)=\text{space} \qquad\qquad \text{[line z2]}$$

This formula is valid only if position (z1,p1) lies before position (z2,p2) or if the two positions are equal (in which case the region in question is empty). I.e., the formula above applies only if (z1=z2 **and** p1≤p2 **or** z1<z2). The values of these variables must, of course, be valid line and position numbers.

nameloc(z,p1,p2): A name begins in position (z,p1) and ends just before position (z,p2) if (1) line z is within the array and (2) a name begins in position (z,p1) and (3) every position from (z,p1) to (z,p2-1) inclusive contains a character other than a space and (4) position (z,p2) does not belong to the name. A name begins in position (z,p1) if position p1 lies within the line and contains a character other than a space and either position (z,p1) is the first position in the line or the previous position contains a space. Position (z,p2) does not belong to the name if it either does not lie within the line or contains a space:

$1 \leq z \leq n$ **and** $1 \leq p1 < p2 \leq \text{length}(A(z))+1$ [ranges of z, p1, p2]

and $(p1=1$ [beginning of line]

  or $1 < p1$ **and** $\text{mid}(A(z),p1-1,1)=\text{space})$
                                      [space before (z,p1)]

and $\displaystyle\mathop{}_{p=p1}^{p2-1}\ \text{mid}(A(z),p,1)\neq\text{space}$ [no space in name]

and $(p2=\text{length}(A(z))+1$ [end of line]

  or $p2 \leq \text{length}(A(z))$ **and** $\text{mid}(A(z),p2,1)=\text{space})$
                                      [space in (z,p2)]

This expression can be simplified somewhat: after each **or**, the subexpressions "$1 < p1$ **and**" and "$p2 \leq \text{length}(A(z))$ **and**" may be left out. If it can be guaranteed elsewhere that only valid line and position numbers are generated for z and p1 respectively, then "$1 \leq z$" and "$1 \leq p1$" may also be left out.

5.4.2 (3). Note that the term "inside" as used here is not really precise. Task descriptions formulated in a natural language are often ambiguous, sometimes even misleading. Frequently one notices this and discovers the actually intended meaning only when one tries to translate the description into another language. The most stringent test arises when the target language allows only precise, unambiguous statements.

In this case the only reasonable interpretation of the requirement is as follows: Position (bl,bp) may not be part of a name which began in a previous position.

Position (bl,bp) would be in a name which began earlier if and only if it and the immediately previous position each contain a character other than a space:

$1 \leq bl \leq n$ **and** $1 \leq bp-1$ **and** $bp \leq \text{length}(A(bl))$
and $\text{mid}(A(bl),bp-1,1)\neq\text{space}$ **and** $\text{mid}(A(bl),bp,1)\neq\text{space}$

The desired condition is the negation of the above expression. After simplifying, it is:

bl=n+1 **or** bp=1 **or** bp=length(A(bl))+1
or mid(A(bl),bp-1,1)=space **or** mid(A(bl),bp,1)=space

In contrast to the sentence "position (bl,bp) does not lie inside a name", the above mathematical formulation of the condition is unambiguous and subject to only one interpretation.

A.3. Every identity can be proved by listing all combinations of the possible values of the variables x, y and z together with the corresponding values of the expressions in question, i.e. by completing a "truth table". Alternatively, many identities can be proved by applying previously verified identities.

There are four possible combinations of the values of two Boolean (logical) variables. For three variables there are eight possible combinations of their values:

false	false	false
false	false	true
false	true	false
false	true	true
true	false	false
true	false	true
true	true	false
true	true	true

A.4 (1). F = [(B **and** C) **or** (**not** B **and** D)]. It can be easily shown that this expression satisfies the given definition of F by completing a truth table.

A.4 (2). [x **and** y $\Longrightarrow$ x]

=

[**not** (x **and** y) **or** x]

=

[**not** x **or** **not** y **or** x]

=

[true **or** **not** y]

=

true

[x $\Longrightarrow$ x **or** y]

=

[not x or x or y]
=
true

Alternatively, the statements can be proved by constructing truth tables.

A.4 (3). [x and (y or z)]
=
[x and x and (y or z)]
=
[x and (x and y or x and z)]
=
[x and (x and x and y or x and z)]
=
[x and x and (x and y or z)]
=
[x and (x and y or z)]

The expression in the third line above also equals:

[x and (x and y or x and x and z)]
=
[x and x and (y or x and z)]
=
[x and (y or x and z)]

The first and last expressions are equal by identity 5 in Appendix A, section A.3.

A.4 (4). It is given that a implies x and b implies y. If both a and b are true, then both x and y are true, i.e. (x and y) is true. If either a or b is true, then x or y respectively is true and hence (x or y) is true.

More formally, we wish first to show that

[(a ⟹ x) and (b ⟹ y)] ⟹ [a and b ⟹ x and y]

This expression can be transformed as follows:

[(not a or x) and (not b or y)]
⟹ [not a or not b or x and y]
=
not [(not a or x) and (not b or y)]
or [not a or not b or x and y]

=
a **and not** x **or** b **and not** y
or not a **or not** b **or** x **and** y
=   [Appendix A, section A.3, identity 17]
not x **or not** y **or not** a **or not** b **or** y
=

true

The second part of the problem,

$$[(a \implies x) \text{ and } (b \implies y)] \implies [a \text{ or } b \implies x \text{ or } y]$$

can be formally proved in the same way.

A.4 (5).
1. [x **and** (**not** y **or** z)] = [x **and not** y **or** x **and** z]
2. [x **or not** y **or** z]
3. [**not** x **or not** y **or** z]
4. [**not** x **and not** y **or** z]
5. $a \neq 0$
6. true
7. false
8. $a = 0$

A.5 (1). For the **and** series:

$$[\text{and}_{i=1}^{n} A(i)]$$
=
$$[\text{true and}_{i=1}^{n} A(i)]$$
=
$$[(n<1 \text{ or } n \geq 1) \text{ and}_{i=1}^{n} A(i)]$$
=
$$[n<1 \text{ and}_{i=1}^{n} A(i) \text{ or } n \geq 1 \text{ and}_{i=1}^{n} A(i)]$$
=
$$[n<1 \text{ or } n \geq 1 \text{ and}_{i=1}^{n} A(i)]$$
=
$$[n<1 \text{ or } n \geq 1 \text{ and } A(n) \text{ and}_{i=1}^{n-1} A(i)]$$

The corresponding derivation for the **or** series is similar:

$$[\text{or}_{i=1}^{n} A(i)]$$
=
$$[\text{true and } (\text{or}_{i=1}^{n} A(i))]$$
=

$[(n < 1 \text{ or } n \geq 1) \text{ and } (\text{or}_{i=1}^{n} A(i))]$

$=$

$[n < 1 \text{ and } (\text{or}_{i=1}^{n} A(i)) \text{ or } n \geq 1 \text{ and } (\text{or}_{i=1}^{n} A(i))]$

$=$

$[n < 1 \text{ and false or } n \geq 1 \text{ and } (\text{or}_{i=1}^{n} A(i))]$

$=$

$[n \geq 1 \text{ and } (\text{or}_{i=1}^{n} A(i))]$

$=$

$[n \geq 1 \text{ and } (A(n) \text{ or}_{i=1}^{n-1} A(i))]$

BIBLIOGRAPHY

Alagić, Suad; Arbib, Michael A., *The Design of Well-Structured and Correct Programs*, Springer-Verlag, New York, Heidelberg, Berlin, 1978.

Baber, Robert L., *Software Reflected: The Socially Responsible Programming of Our Computers*, North-Holland Publishing Co., Amsterdam, New York, Oxford, 1982.

Baber, Robert L., *Softwarereflexionen: Ideen und Konzepte für die Praxis*, Springer-Verlag, Berlin, Heidelberg, New York, 1986.

Baber, Robert L., *The Spine of Software: Designing Provably Correct Software – Theory and Practice*, John Wiley & Sons, Chichester, 1987.

Backhouse, Roland C., *Program Construction and Verification*, Prentice-Hall International, Englewood Cliffs, N. J., 1986.

Bauer, Friedrich L.; Wössner, Hans, *Algorithmische Sprache und Programmentwicklung*, Springer-Verlag, Berlin, Heidelberg, New York, 1984.

Dahl, O.-J.; Dijkstra, E. W.; Hoare, C. A. R., *Structured Programming*, Academic Press, London, 1972.

Denvir, Tim, *Introduction to Discrete Mathematics for Software Engineering*, Macmillan Education, Basingstoke, 1986.

Dijkstra, Edsger W., *A Discipline of Programming*, Prentice-Hall, Inc., Englewood Cliffs, N. J., 1976.

Futschek, Gerald, *Programmentwicklung und Verifikation*, Springer-Verlag, Wien, New York, 1989.

Grams, Timm, *Denkfallen und Programmierfehler*, Springer-Verlag, Berlin, Heidelberg, 1990.

Gries, David, *The Science of Programming*, Springer-Verlag, New York, Heidelberg, Berlin, 1981.

Hoare, C. A. R., *Communicating Sequential Processes*, Prentice-Hall International, Englewood Cliffs, N. J., 1985.

IEEE Spectrum, "Lethal dose", in Faults & Failures column, Vol. 24, No. 12, 1987 December, S. 16.

Jones, Cliff B., *Systematic Software Development Using VDM*, Prentice Hall International, Englewood Cliffs, N.J., 1986.

Joyce, Ed, "Software Bugs: A Matter of Life and Liability", *Datamation*, 1987 May 15, S. 88-92.

Linger, Richard C.; Mills, Harlan D.; Witt, Bernard I., *Structured Programming: Theory and Practice*, Addison-Wesley Publishing Co., Reading, Massachusetts, 1979.

Loeckx, Jacques; Sieber, Kurt, *The Foundations of Program Verification*, B. G. Teubner, Stuttgart, and John Wiley & Sons, Chichester, 1984.

McGowan, Clement L.; Kelly, John R., *Top-Down Structured Programming Techniques*, Petrocelli/Charter, New York, 1975.

Spivey, J.M., *The Z Notation*, Prentice Hall, New York, 1989.

Thomas, Martyn, *Should we trust computers?*, The BCS/UNISYS Annual Lecture 1988, 1988 July 4, British Computer Society, London.

INDEX

Task Analysis